Praise for ENOUGH

"A SCATHING CATEGORY-5 HURRICANE OF A BOOK cajoling and scolding many in the black community for their systematic lack of economic progress over the past several decades." —*Indianapolis Star*

"Cosby's spirit and energizing candor courses through an important new book—Juan Williams's *Enough*. . . . Williams's rallying cry 'Enough' WOULD HAVE GLADDENED THE HEART OF MY FRIEND THE LATE BAYARD RUSTIN, a key strategist for Dr. Martin Luther King Jr."
—Nat Hentoff,
Washington Times

"In a fluid prose style . . . Williams exhorts so-called black leaders to return to the days when leadership had meaning and purpose beyond corporate shake-downs, scandals, and outdated rants about the sins of white people. . . . Straying from the party line seems to be the only taboo left in black America. . . . WILLIAMS BREAKS THROUGH THE TABOO AND OFFERS COM-MONSENSE ADVICE AND SOLUTIONS."
—LaShawn Barber,
Washington Examiner

"Bill Cosby famously has spoken out about the cultural problems that hold African Americans back more than racism or other structural obstacles. NPR's Juan Williams has added intellectual heft to Cosby's argument with his new book *Enough*. THESE ARE BRAVE MEN."
—Rich Lowry,
New York Post

"I HIGHLY RECOMMEND *ENOUGH* to those who are really interested in knowing our nation's history, and specifically the odyssey of African Americans in this country. Juan Williams has, through Bill Cosby, spoken for the quiet majority of African Americans who desperately look for some voice to articulate what they know is truth."
—Douglas Wilder,
mayor of Richmond, Virginia,
and former governor of Virginia

ENOUGH

The Phony Leaders, Dead-End Movements, and

Culture of Failure That Are Undermining Black

America—and What We Can Do About It

JUAN WILLIAMS

THREE RIVERS PRESS
NEW YORK

Published in the United States by Three Rivers Press, an imprint of the
Crown Publishing Group, a division of Random House, Inc., New York.
www.crownpublishing.com

Three Rivers Press and the Tugboat design are registered trademarks
of Random House, Inc.
Originally published in hardcover in the United States by Crown Publishers,
an imprint of the Crown Publishing Group, a division of Random House, Inc.,
New York, in 2006.

Library of Congress Cataloging-in-Publication Data

Williams, Juan.
Enough : the phony leaders, dead-end movements, and culture of failure
that are undermining Black America— and what we can do about it /
Juan Williams.
p. cm.
1. African American leadership.   2. African Americans—Social conditions—
1975–   3. African Americans—Politics and government.   4. United States—
Race relations.   5. Racism—United States.   I. Title.
E185.615W49155   2006
973'.0496073—dc22
2006002987
ISBN: 978-0-307-33824-2

Printed in the United States of America

Design by Lenny Henderson

10 9 8 7 6 5

First Paperback Edition

This book is dedicated to the people rising above Katrina's storm in the city of New Orleans, the Gulf Coast, and across America.

And the Lord said . . . "I will judge his house for ever for the iniquity which he knoweth; because his sons made themselves vile, and he restrained them not."

—1 SAMUEL 3:11–13

CONTENTS

ENOUGH

INTRODUCTION

I N 2006, JUST AFTER THE January holiday honoring Dr. Martin Luther King Jr., an animated Dr. King came to life on the Cartoon Network's new show *The Boondocks*. Animator Aaron McGruder had created an older version of the assassinated civil rights legend. He stood at the pulpit of a black church, looking out at gangster rappers in a fistfight, high school dropouts calling each other "niggers," and unmarried black teenage mothers dressed like whores. "Is this it? This is what I got all those ass-whippings for?—I had a dream once," he said, referring to the sacrifices he made during the civil rights struggles of the fifties and sixties. King's face twisted with disappointment. His voice dripped with disdain for what had come of his dream.

Every word of the cartoon Dr. King's stinging sermon was rooted in an electric speech that actor and comedian Bill Cosby had given in 2004 on the fiftieth anniversary of the U.S. Supreme Court's decision in *Brown v. Board of Education of Topeka*. Much as W.E.B. DuBois predicted the problem of the "colorline" would dominate the twentieth century, Cosby's speech set the agenda for civil rights in the twenty-first century by calling for the most powerful, self-reliant black Americans in history to deal with the crisis of children without parents, children failing in school, and civil rights leaders making excuses for absurdly high rates of crime in the black community. It was a speech that continues to redefine discussions of race, poverty, and class in America.

1

*   *   *

THE EVENT WAS GOLD-PLATED. On May 17, 2004, three thousand of black America's elite, in tuxedos and gowns, gathered at Constitution Hall in Washington, D.C. The very building where black opera star Marian Anderson had been barred from singing in 1939 because of her race filled up with elegantly attired black people for a celebration of the golden anniversary of the *Brown* decision, the crowning moment in the midcentury African American struggle for racial equality. It was exactly fifty years earlier, on May 17, 1954, that the Supreme Court stunned the nation by ordering racial integration of public schools in *Brown*.

The featured speaker for the anniversary gala was the famed entertainer Bill Cosby. He had a script for his remarks but he didn't use it. The result was a speech that created a roaring controversy about the state of life in black America fifty years after *Brown*.

Oseola McCarty didn't live to hear the Cosby speech. But her voice echoed in every moment. The speech was simply the latest version of an anthem to the virtue of struggle and the belief that we shall overcome. Just before she died, McCarty told an interviewer: If you want to feel proud of yourself, then do good. Take action that will make you proud. Black or white, don't make excuses, don't blame anyone, and if you really want to feel proud, then do something to help someone else.

The end of segregated schools had come too late for Ms. McCarty. By the end of third grade in her rundown school in segregated Hattiesburg, Mississippi, the nine-year-old's family pulled her out of classes. She washed other people's dirty clothes all her life and then the "Little Colored Lady" in the Mississippi Delta gave her entire life savings of $150,000 for college scholarships aimed at black students. The example of an eighty-seven-year-old third-grade dropout using her small pocketbook to open school doors for the next generation of black children drew national attention. People called her a strong, determined, and sacrificing soul, a living black American saint.

At her life's end, she said, the prize she wanted most of all was that the "children won't have to work so hard like I did." More than six hundred other people were moved by McCarty's example to add to the scholarship money she gave the University of Southern Mississippi. In her actions, black and white Americans saw the best of African American traditions come alive—the tradition of defying the odds to overcome and help others get over. President Clinton called her to the White House and gave her the Presidential Citizens Medal—the second-highest honor a president can give an American civilian. Harvard University gave her an honorary degree. The United Nations held a special ceremony to honor her. Media mogul Ted Turner said he felt compelled to act by the example of the "the little colored lady washer who gave away everything." Inspired by McCarty, Turner gave a billion dollars to charity. Five years after she died, sixteen young people had already had their education paid for by "Mama O's" act of grace.

McCarty was no educator. But her actions put her in a long tradition of black people striving to open school doors for black children and succeeding despite the seemingly insurmountable barriers of racial oppression and poverty. Black women such as Harriet Tubman, Nannie Helen Burroughs, and Mary McLeod Bethune all created schools to educate slaves and their children. They acted to lift a veil of ignorance from people who had been held down, condemned to slavery, and denied the chance to learn to read and write, thus limiting them to working as unskilled, cheap laborers. McCarty energized the legacy of uplift by lending a helping hand to the next generation in a new era. Her action in helping others was in line with such seemingly disparate black activists as Frederick Douglass, Booker T. Washington, W.E.B. DuBois, Marcus Garvey, A. Philip Randolph, Thurgood Marshall, Martin Luther King Jr., and Malcolm X. Despite their wildly different political philosophies, all of these leaders understood that all hope for progress began with self-help, education, and decisive action.

Cosby's speech never mentioned Oseola McCarty, but in many ways it spoke in her voice. Cosby called on black Americans to keep their self-help traditions alive. His speech challenged black people to take a hard look at poor parenting and the cultural rot preventing too many black children from throwing off the veil of ignorance covering them, a situation rooted in twenty-first-century problems of poverty, disproportionate fatherlessness, bad schools, high rates of unemployment, and lives wasted in jails.

Of course, if McCarty had been alive to praise the substance of Cosby's message, she might have been harshly questioned. Hip critics wise to the street life surely would have dismissed her as "country" and old. They might have asked if she was "authentically black," and pointed out that she knew nothing about "thug life" or "keeping it real." Her humble, striving, up-from-the-bootstraps approach might have been attacked as pretentious, the tactics of a black woman who forgot where she came from, an Uncle Tom or Aunt Jemima. That's what happened to Cosby.

The Supreme Court's 1954 *Brown* decision was as large an event in American history as the Civil War. The war, fought to prevent slavery from dividing the union, ended in 1865, almost a century before *Brown*. Making the former slaves full citizens of the Republic in the aftermath of the great war created political and cultural divisions that tore at the ideals of a nation based on a

Declaration of Independence, which articulated the principle of all men being created equally with "unalienable rights . . . life, liberty, and the pursuit of happiness." Black Americans, however, even as free people, endured second-class citizenship that required amendments to the U.S. Constitution to make them full citizens and protect their rights, liberty, and ability to vote and own property under the law. Even then, a culture of segregation and intimidation, from cross burnings to lynching, gave birth to laws that forced black Americans to live as a lower caste. They attended separate and inferior schools, ate separately, shopped separately, and often lived in fear and submission to the power of white racial domination. The Supreme Court's 1954 decision was a mighty break with that past.

"In these days it is doubtful that any child may reasonably be expected to succeed in life if he is denied the opportunity of an education," Chief Justice Earl Warren said that day as he read from the decision that marked a sudden departure from the nation's history of slavery and legal segregation premised on inferiority. "To separate [black children] from others of similar age and qualifications solely because of their race generates a feeling of inferiority as to their status in the community. . . . We conclude that in the field of public education the doctrine of 'separate but equal' has no place."

The *Brown* decision was a signal moment in twentieth-century American life that ignited the beginning of the end for legal, state-supported segregation in American life. It set in motion the greatest social movement in all of American history, the modern civil rights movement. *Brown* gave birth to Rosa Parks's successful fight against segregated seating on Montgomery, Alabama, buses in 1955 only a year later. The *Brown* ruling forced President Eisenhower to send federal troops to protect nine black children who wanted to go to Little Rock's Central High School in 1957. It was the idea of race-blind justice at the heart of *Brown* that stirred idealism on college campuses and in churches and union halls. *Brown* set the stage for the 1963 March on Washington, the 1964 Civil Rights Act, and the 1965 Voting Rights Act. All of this change flowed from the seminal ruling in *Brown*. Martin Luther King's dream of the children of slave owners and slave masters working together, as well as Malcolm X's defiant calling out of racial hypocrites, is rooted in the *Brown* decision's clarifying vision of an America where racial inequality was deemed illegal, unconstitutional, and at odds with the principles of the country. And *Brown* is the seed of higher secondary school and college graduation rates for blacks and Latinos in the second half of the twentieth century. The roots of the largest, most politically powerful black middle class in American history are in the *Brown* case.

So, on the fiftieth anniversary of *Brown*, the elite of the most highly educated and most affluent black people in world history came together to celebrate. In keeping with the gala atmosphere, Hollywood celebrities mixed with politicians and the rich. The leaders of major black civil rights groups—the NAACP, the National Council of Negro Women, and the NAACP Legal Defense and Education Fund—were all on stage. Awards were presented to elderly lawyers who had played roles in the *Brown* case such as ninety-seven-year-old Oliver Hill of Richmond, Virginia. But the most highly anticipated speaker for the night was Bill Cosby.

"The Cos," as he is known by Americans who regularly put him on their list of the most admired people in the country, is renowned for his generosity. The sixty-nine-year-old star has given more than $20 million to black colleges. He starred in a groundbreaking TV show that presented, for the very first time, an upper-middle-class black family as completely free of self-hate or pathology. The Huxtables happily confronted the ironies and absurdities of modern American life without a preoccupation with race. It was the most popular program on American television for several seasons. Both the TV character and the real Cosby embodied the ideal that had driven the architects of the *Brown* decision. Able to compete and succeed in an integrated society, Cosby (and Cliff Huxtable) asserted his birthright as a full-blooded member of the American family, while never ignoring his identity as a black man steeped in African American culture.

Who better to lead the hallelujah chorus for the big anniversary than the man who personified centuries of dreams come to life—the dream of black people succeeding in the American mainstream? He was expected to be a safe choice. All that was asked of him was that he tell a few tasteful jokes, be properly reverent of the civil rights leaders on stage, and offer admiring words to the old folks who had been heroes in the making of the *Brown* case fifty years earlier.

Instead, Bill Cosby got mad.

"Ladies and gentlemen, these people—they opened doors, they gave us the right[s]," he said, praising the lawyers and educators present. "But today, ladies and gentlemen, in our cities we have fifty-percent dropout [rates among young black men] in our neighborhoods. We have [the highest percentage of any American racial group with] men in prison. No longer is a person embarrassed because [she is] pregnant without a husband. No longer is a boy considered an embarrassment if he tries to run away from being the father. . . .

"Ladies and gentlemen, the lower economic and low middle economic people are not holding their end in this deal."

The crowd was caught off guard. Emotionally they were set to laugh politely with Cosby. But this was no comedy routine. It was edgy, high-wire political commentary about a real crisis. Cosby dared to explain why some black Americans turned their backs on the opportunities created by the struggles and sacrifices of generations past. He was willing to assign blame and point fingers. No one came to the anniversary gala to be chastised or reminded of failures. Most of the audience was not sure if the humorist was joking, so initially there was lots of laughter. After all, this was Cosby, black America's lovable funny man, speaking at an invitation-only event. People kept laughing at what they thought might be jokes. But then people began to offer up "Amen" and applause even as Cosby continued delivering a sharp critique of contemporary black American life. By mid-speech it was clear that Cosby had pushed the line past humor.

"You can't keep asking Jesus [to do] this for you. You can't keep asking that God will find a way. God is tired of you," he said skating out of line and long past any reverence for the power of the Christian church in black America. And he kept going. Next he said the problems weighing down black America fifty years after *Brown* had nothing to do with white people or the racism that clamped chains on slaves. "We can't blame white people," he said. Then he added: "*Brown v. Board* is no longer the white person's problem." And now, way past the bounds of the expectations of the happy crowd, Cosby said that for all their success in breaking down barriers to equal opportunity in America, "you wouldn't know that anybody had done a damned thing." He cited the high dropout rate as well as the disproportionate number of black children born into poverty as the babies of young, single mothers. (According to the National Center for Health Statistics, in 2004, 69.2 percent of black children were born to unwed mothers. That contrasts with 24.5 percent for white children and approximately 45 percent for Hispanic children.) Thumping the lectern, the now-not-so-funny man said black parents buy five-hundred-dollar sneakers for their kids, but won't spend a dime on the Hooked on Phonics program to teach those kids how to read. "Thank God," he proclaimed, that people who spent their lives breaking down segregation so that black people could have a chance for success don't "know what is going on today."

On a righteous roll, Cosby turned his anger to excuses made to explain why American jails are filled with black men. "These are not political [prisoners]," he said. "These are people going around stealing Coca-Cola. People getting shot in the back of the head over a piece of pound cake! Then we all run out and are outraged [saying], 'The cops shouldn't have shot him.' What the hell was he doing with the pound cake in his hand?"

Cosby's speech took flight as powerful, blunt, public talk about issues that most black people, middle-class or poor, speak about only privately with other black people and far from microphones. He didn't dress up his thoughts in statistical data. He didn't attribute any conclusions to academic sources or sociological theorists. He just took the weight of making the charges about the failures of black people on his black shoulders, and he made especially stinging observations about black youth culture:

- "People putting their clothes on backwards—isn't that a sign of something going on wrong? Aren't you paying attention? People with their hats on backwards, pants down around the crack . . . are you waiting for Jesus to pull his pants up? Isn't it a sign of something when she's got her dress all the way up to the crack. . . ?"

- "We are not Africans. Those people are not Africans; they don't know a damned thing about Africa. With names like

Shaniqua, Shaligua, Mohammed and all that crap and all of them are in jail."

• "Everybody knows it's important to speak English except these knuckleheads. You can't land a plane with 'Why you ain't . . .' You can't be a doctor with that kind of crap coming out of your mouth. There is no Bible that has that kind of language. Where did these people get the idea that they're moving ahead on this . . . these people are fighting hard to be ignorant."

• "Five or six different children—same woman, eight, ten different husbands or whatever. Pretty soon you're going to have to have DNA cards so you can tell who you're making love to . . . you could have sex with your grandmother . . . you keep those numbers coming, I'm just predicting."

Now, what was most impressive about the response to these sharp, even nasty riffs on the self-defeating habits of many young black people, and the bad job black parents did in raising them, was that there was not one call for Cosby to sit down. No one shouted out for him to shut up. In fact, Cosby at one point had to ask the audience to stop interrupting his rants with clapping, loud shouts of praise, and spiraling, singsong amens. "No more applause," he finally said.

To an only slightly quieter audience, he then began challenging black people's inaction about crime in black America, condemning tolerance for crack houses and drive-by shootings. He asked why the Christian churches had nothing to say about criminals dominating black neighborhoods. Now Cosby came to a damning conclusion: "What the hell good is *Brown v. Board of Ed-*

ucation if nobody wants it?" Earlier that night he had received an award for advancing educational opportunities for black Americans. As he began to finish up his speech, he thanked the NAACP for the award, and upped the ante one more time. This time he spoke for all the old-timers who had been lawyers on the *Brown* case, the people who had sent donations to support the lawyers, and the social scientists who had done research to support the call for integrated schools.

"They've got to wonder what the hell happened. *Brown v. Board of Education*—these people who marched and were hit in the face with rocks and punched in the face to get an education and [today] we got these knuckleheads walking around who don't want to learn English . . . these people are not funny anymore. And that's not my brother. And that's not my sister. They're faking and they're dragging me down because the state, the city . . . have to pick up the tab on them because they don't want to accept that they have to study to get an education. . . .

"*Brown v. Board of Education*—where are we today . . . the white man, he's laughing—got to be laughing. Fifty percent dropout [rate]—rest of them in prison."

THE IMMEDIATE REACTION TO COSBY that night was a standing ovation. Kweisi Mfume, executive director of the NAACP, later said none of the civil rights activists on stage knew how to follow such a radical, unscripted presentation. He wasn't sure what to say about what he had just heard, but the look on his face suggested that he was jazzed by Cosby's decision to take a risk and offer himself to Black America as modern prophet. He might as well have said that no one can control Bill Cosby. And then Mfume could have added that nobody takes a stand-up comic all that seriously, anyway. Some who were backstage said the applause was for Bill Cosby the legendary entertainer, and not for the amateur social critic. But there was no apology that night from civil rights leaders. Cosby offered no follow-up qualifications or explanations. The audience reacted with genuine pleasure to a biting but at times hilarious and intimate riff on us—black folks.

A few days later, however, a short news item appeared in the gossip section of the *Washington Post* about the buzz being generated by word-of-mouth accounts of Cosby's speech. It said some people, including some of the civil rights luminaries at the event, thought Cosby had maligned poor black people, that he was blaming America's most vulnerable population for their problems. That prompted a round of newspaper and TV stories about what Cosby said. Few dismissed Cosby as a comedian doing a routine, or as a lightweight intellectual who had made a fool of himself by going off the deep end in front of a big crowd. Instead, his comments about blacks needing to take personal responsibility for their children, for crime, and local schools, gained power as they were echoed by the Washington, D.C., police chief and even politicians such as Jesse Jackson. The street corner wisdom among blacks and whites, apart from whether Cosby was right or wrong, was that he had been courageous in calling by name a serious problem that most people found too dicey to talk about in public. Columnists and talk-radio shows joined the now-weighty discussion about Cosby's "Pound Cake Speech."

Then the critics mounted their attack. Theodore Shaw, the head of the NAACP Legal Defense Fund, wrote a serious analysis of the Pound Cake Speech in a column in the *Washington Post*. In Shaw's view, Cosby had demonized poor black people while ignoring "systemic issues of race and racism" that continued to limit the progress of black people. As the man who spoke immediately after

Cosby finished his remarks at Constitution Hall, Shaw said he knew "even before I reached the stage that Cosby's comments would be hijacked by those who pretend that racism is no longer an issue and who view poor black people with disdain." The lawyer, heir to the legacy of Thurgood Marshall and the architects of the *Brown* decision, recounted a recent Texas case he had handled, in which a corrupt undercover policeman had lied about finding drugs on black people and sent many of them to jail. He scored Cosby again when he wrote that a black African immigrant, Amadou Diallo, who did not have a gun and was not stealing pound cake, was shot forty-one times by New York City police.

Shaw also reported that he had phoned Cosby a few days after the speech to personally express his distaste. He said while they disagreed on much about what Cosby said that night, they agreed on a middle ground. They'd jointly fight racism as well as patterns of negative, self-defeating behavior by black people. What was curious was Shaw's inclination to compromise. Cosby had broken with the civil rights establishment's orthodoxy of portraying blacks as victims. That was the reason no other modern black leader or personality had previously pointed out the obvious problems bedeviling black America. Cosby had broken the code of silence, leaving himself wide open to be slammed. But Shaw, as a leading voice for the gray-haired rebels of the civil rights movement, apparently didn't feel free to blast Cosby as an "Uncle Tom." Cosby was too popular with blacks, not to mention whites, to be excommunicated from the civil rights establishment. As much as they wanted to throttle him, the old guard couldn't afford to kill this messenger. "The issue of personal responsibility is real," Kweisi Mfume told a reporter. "A lot of people didn't want him to say what he said because it was an open forum. But if the truth be told, he was on target."

So it was left to black academics and self-styled black radicals to pick up the attack. Cosby was not their hero, on TV or in person. The starting point for the critics was that he should not have said it in public, on the fiftieth anniversary of the *Brown* decision. And he really shouldn't have said it without explaining to white people—especially conservative white people—that he wasn't talking about all black people, but just some black people. Author Earl Ofari Hutchinson wrote in the *Los Angeles Times* that "Cosby didn't invent the shopworn stereotype that poor blacks are their own worst enemy . . . but what [people] heard from him only reinforces negative beliefs about the poor." In a black paper, the *Los Angeles Sentinel*, a writer named Larry Ashby accused Cosby of "callous insensitivity." The bottom line, Ashby wrote, was that Cosby's "tirade failed to cite racism and related systemic factors that clearly provide the context for poor education, excessive poverty, violence, and hopelessness. Bill Cosby surely knows that minimizing the continuing impact of race is too dangerous a game for blacks to engage in."

A black University of Pennsylvania professor, Michael Eric Dyson, condemned Cosby's comments as evidence of "classist, elitist viewpoints . . . that only reinforce suspicions about black humanity." White-run TV shows, hungry for a glimpse of a fight inside black American leadership, put those critics on camera to take their shots at Cosby. Michael Males, a sociologist, argued that Cosby had few statistics to support his fierce opinions. If the comedian used statistics honestly, Males said, he would have had to talk about recent declines in teen pregnancy, violent crime, and spousal abuse among black people. Males said Cosby ignored the fact that there are now more black Americans in college than at any other time in history.

In the *Village Voice*, Ta-Nehisi Coates said Cosby was guilty of directing "invective" against black people that normally would prompt the NAACP to start boycotts and picketing. He said no white person could get away with a speech attacking low-income blacks, maybe not even a black person could get away with it, with one exception. That exception, he said, was Cosby. Coates argued that Cosby was insulated from proper rebuke because of his long history of giving money to black organizations and politicians. He concluded, however, that Cosby was just another old man "showing his age." He wrote that Cosby was "no more insightful than your crotchety old uncle standing on the corner shaking his cane, ranting to no one in particular: 'Damn kids!' Of course, no one in his or her right mind would hand your uncle a bullhorn."

One of the few white writers to take on Cosby was a cynical Barbara Ehrenreich. In a column in the *New York Times*, she explained that she almost missed the controversy over Cosby's comments because it was another billionaire bashing poor blacks: "The only thing that gave this particular story a little piquancy is that the billionaire doing the bashing is black himself." She dismissed the whole episode as the latest version of attacks on poor black women as lazy and promiscuous baby machines, and black kids as a "generation of 'super-predators,' gang-bangers, and thugs."

One Cosby critic pointed out that Cosby had once created a lovable but street-wise character, Fat Albert, who sometimes spoke in a black dialect. Yet here he was, criticizing people for engaging in the same kinds of behavior as Fat Albert. Hypocrisy was the bottom line coming from a chorus of critics. Christopher Farley, a *Time* magazine cultural critic, also complained about Cosby scolding young black people for not speaking proper English. Great black writers, ranging from Zora Neale Hurston to Langston Hughes, wrote literature using black dialects. Others noted that Cosby had admitted to having an extramarital affair, but now was condemning the sexual behavior of other people. A range of critics came at Cosby with charges of elitism, contempt for the poor, and insensitivity to the difficulty of getting out of poverty, especially deep poverty that has been in place for generations. For several days, Cosby's comments dominated black talk radio. Joe Madison, the host of a popular syndicated show, heard both sides of the controversy from his mostly black audience, and he came down firmly in opposition. "Cosby went overboard when he absolved white America and the government of any responsibility for the ills of the poor black community. He made it seem like the problems affecting poor black people in the community are pathological. You can't paint the poor black community with a broad brush."

In general, political and social criticism of black people by other black people is a non-starter in America—unless you are a stand-up comic. Even then it can be a problem. When comedian Chris Rock joked that Washington, D.C.'s mostly black population elected a crack addict as mayor ("What I want to know is who he was running against"), his purely comedic performance prompted comments and essays accusing him of being a closet conservative. But harsh criticism of Cosby as not being in touch with issues facing most black people did not play well. He may be an entertainer, but he wasn't smiling when he delivered his lines. Cosby's speech, by virtue of its setting and his stature, rose above social satire. Cosby is at a different level of American life. Cosby the philanthropist, as opposed to Cosby the comedian, walks at the front of black society, alongside the lawyers, doctors, and political leaders. He had to be taken seriously. At the same time, it was hard for critics to label him as part of a racist conspiracy, or, because of his long history of support for progressive causes, to diminish him by putting him in league with racists or opportunistic black conservatives. He wasn't presenting himself to white people as the black man they could trust; he was telling home truths to his own people, out of an authentic, almost shockingly raw sense of despair.

As the criticism from black intellectuals and activists rained down on him, Cosby did not backpedal. He did tell an interviewer that he'd meant to say "some" black people failed to take advantage of newly opened opportunities, but not all black people. But he didn't start stuttering or stumbling, and he never apologized. Instead, he said he had been saying the same thing to black audiences for months; it was only when the white press heard him at the fiftieth-anniversary celebration that the controversy erupted. The implication was that black people had no trouble with his comments. He asked if he was supposed to keep quiet out of concern for white racists who already didn't think much of black people. He said he hadn't directed his comments at Constitution Hall to whites, but had spoken out to black people about the "disease that is infecting our people more and more every day." And he added to one reporter: "After you blame me and decide that Bill Cosby is an elitist . . . watch the dropout rate go up to sixty percent."

As for his criticism of "knuckleheads" who failed to speak proper English, he pointed out that Zora Neal Hurston and Langston Hughes spoke classic English and chose as a matter of art to write in dialect and create scenes of poor black life that had morphed into fascinating subcultures. And he added a sting to the defense by noting that Farley, the *Time* magazine writer, did not write in black dialect in *Time* or speak in black dialect when he voiced his critique on *Good Morning America*.

In making his defense, Cosby portrayed himself as a righteous man who cared for his people and refused to be intimidated by militant blacks who questioned his sincerity, or to be silenced by the chance that some white conservatives would hijack his message for their own purposes: "If I have to make a choice between keeping quiet so that conservative media does not speak negatively, or ringing the bell to galvanize those who want change in the lower economic community, then I choose to be a bell ringer."

The most difficult attack for Cosby to handle was the charge that he had betrayed black America. This line of argument proved hardy, coming to life again and again in news stories, intellectual debate, and on talk radio. It fit with claims that increasing numbers of the growing black middle class wanted nothing to do with the "black underclass." It was a damning image of nouveau-riche blacks, as represented by Cosby, distancing themselves from their poor brothers. Even worse, there was the suggestion that Cosby and his upper-class black friends now felt free to publicly ridicule poor black people. That argument was set forth in a piece in Florida's *Broward Times*, in which Cosby was derided as a spokesman for the black middle class and the "latest in a long line of accommodationist Negro leaders." Authors Glen Ford and Peter Gamble even referred to Cosby's famous speech as evidence of the new, arrogant black middle class that is "sheltered from the real world of zero-sum politics, gentrification, underfunded and abandoned school districts, swelling prison populations, racial profiling, economic marginalization, drug abuse, and other poverty-based social ills."

This response was not exactly unpredictable. In fact, to some degree, it was understandable. As a group, black people are obviously sensitive to any reinforcement of the racist characterization of them as stupid, lazy, violent, and lacking in moral character. Those stereotypes have persisted across the years in minstrel shows and music videos, and have led to a negative self-image. That's why image and role models are more important to black people than to most other Americans. Blacks are concerned about image to the point of paranoia, opening a door for conspiracy theories that blame everything, including AIDS, on malevolent white powers that are out to hold down black people. Thus, for Cosby to air this dirty laundry struck at a sensitive psychic nerve. Nevertheless, he continued.

Three weeks after he ignited the debate, Cosby kept a commitment to appear at the annual convention of Jesse Jackson's Rainbow/PUSH Coalition and Citizenship Education Fund. He was feeling defensive about the charges that he had betrayed the black community by exposing problems of the black poor to the world. Speaking to the Chicago activists, Cosby preempted any attack on those lines: "Let me tell you something. Your dirty laundry gets out of school at two-thirty every day. It's cursing and calling each other nigger as they walk up and down the street. They think they're hip. They can't read; they can't write. They're laughing and giggling and they're going nowhere." And he didn't stop there. Those uneducated black kids grow up to be violent, he said. "You've got to stop beating up your women because you can't find a job, because you didn't want to get an education and now you're [making] minimum wage."

When he was pressed about taking the pressure off white people and continued racism, Cosby got fiery. This is the time to "turn the mirror around," he said. "Because for me it is almost analgesic to talk about what the white man is doing against us. And it keeps a person frozen in their seat, it keeps you frozen in the hole you are sitting in."

His words were greeted with thunderous applause. And it prompted him to go further in his comments about post-1954 generations of black Americans not taking advantage of the doors opened by the civil rights movement. "Dogs, water hoses that tear the bark off trees, Emmett Till . . . and you're going to tell me you are going to drop out of school? You're going to tell me you are going to steal from a store?"

Cosby's remarks at the PUSH event made front-page news nationwide. People who might have thought that he was misquoted earlier, or that his words had been taken out of context, now realized that he really had critiqued poor black people. He told one reporter he had no plans to "soften my message," because negative indicators in the black community, from teen pregnancies to illiteracy, were at "epidemic" levels. The black political establishment that had reveled in Cosby's philanthropy and fame felt trapped. The essence of the negative behavior he was railing against was behavior that the NAACP, the black church, the Jesse Jackson activists, and the black intellectuals had long ago decided not to address. Not one civil rights group took up Cosby's call for marches and protests against drug dealers, pregnant teens, deadbeat dads, and hate-filled rap music that celebrates violence. He was now officially a renegade from the black establishment. The only saving grace was that he had built up such a deep reservoir of goodwill that the official black leadership still didn't launch a public attack. They simply ignored him.

Cosby was insulated from a full-fledged assault for several reasons. He was not white, not a conservative, had not grown up middle-class, and was not married to a white woman. As an actor, he had always portrayed positive, smart, successful black people. He had put his personal fortune into advancing black education and had always been a friend to other black people in the sensitive fight over black image in America. He had touched all the bases used by the judges of black racial authority. Essentially, he had a get-out-of-jail pass. But even though he had that goodwill in the bank, no civil rights group lent their credibility to his crusade. The only question was how long it could last, and how far he could go, before broaching too great a taboo.

Without the platform provided by civil rights groups, Cosby announced that he planned a series of town-hall meetings in cities with large black populations, to repeat his message in front of poor black people. At one of the first, in Newark, New Jersey, at New Hope Baptist Church, Cosby was asked why he wasn't talking to white people about holding down black people. "You can't blame white people for everything wrong in your life. . . . What white man made you write a record calling black women bitches and whores?" he shouted at one point. Even more acutely, Cosby began insisting that black Americans, including the poorest of the poor, stop pretending that they lacked money, freedom, and the political skills to handle their own problems. There was silence when he said: "There are people that want you to remain in a hole, and they rejoice in your hopelessness because they have jobs mismanaging you. However, the solution is not becoming victims. We have to rise up and fight on all levels to succeed."

Now Cosby was calling out the old guard that had invited him to Constitution Hall to celebrate their victory in *Brown*—the graying civil rights leadership and the black politicians who stand as the gatekeepers of ideas and attitudes in black popular culture. Who else are the people who "have jobs mismanaging you"? Cosby had thrown down a challenge. He was on the offensive and gaining attention for taking risks in challenging the troubled status quo in black America.

Suddenly, Cosby hit a wall.

His energetic charge was blunted when he found himself charged with the kind of bad behavior he was criticizing in other people. A young woman said Cosby had taken her to his mansion outside Philadelphia, drugged her, and then fondled her breasts and touched her genitals while she was unconscious. Cosby immediately shut down his tour. Then a second woman, a white California lawyer, went to newspapers with a similar charge. She claimed that when she had been trying to break into acting in the 1970s, she'd met Cosby and gone out to dinner with him. After the meal, she alleged, she'd suddenly found herself groggy after taking a pill he gave her, and facing him with his pants down. She said she'd had to fight with him to get him out of her apartment. "I'm not suing him for money," she later told reporters. "I would have waited my natural life if he hadn't drugged another person." A town-hall meeting in Cleveland had to be canceled in January 2005 because Cosby was fighting for his reputation.

Everywhere he went, the issue reporters wanted to discuss was his sexual behavior; his fight with crippling behavior patterns in black America was buried under that heap of dung. A month after the allegations surfaced, the Montgomery County, Pennsylvania, district attorney decided not to file charges of sexual assault against the comedian. The DA said there was insufficient evidence. But the bad publicity left its mark, especially when combined with a previous episode in which Cosby had admitted to an affair outside of his marriage and paying to support the woman's child. Now Cosby was attacked with glee by critics like Professor Dyson. The professor skewered Cosby as a hypocrite; he dismissed his contributions as an actor, an author, and a comedian. He said Cosby's work as a philanthropist did not entitle him to be free of criticism. Cosby personified a black middle class, Dyson argued, that had "lost its mind," and lost touch with history and poor black people. Cosby was still rich, famous, and able to command a microphone. But the clarity of his message was gone with all this static in the air and a unique moment in contemporary civil rights seemed lost.

But even if he was a flawed messenger—and inexact about statistics in his presentation of the message—Cosby had been on to a real issue. Oseola McCarty lived the truth he spoke. Cosby had the spirit of Frederick Douglass and Booker T. Washington and Mary McLeod Bethune in his mouth when he began speaking against lost opportunities in modern black America and the accepted wisdom, fifty years after the *Brown* decision set fire to the great civil rights movement, that black people are victims.

And, most powerfully, the truth backed him up. Skyrocketing rates of black people in jail or locked into an achievement gap in schools, low rates of wealth formation, and low life expectancy are all facts for black America. In March 2006, the *New York Times* reported on its front page that a "huge pool of poorly educated black men are becoming ever more disconnected from mainstream society and to a far greater degree than comparable white or Hispanic men." Most damning of all is the acceptance of the idea that black people are weak and powerless, victims of American society instead of heroes who prove the virtue of America's promise of justice for all. Cosby struck an important blow against the knee-jerk defense of destructive elements in contemporary black culture. He was on the verge of reclaiming the strength black America had in its heritage of overcoming even the worst of slavery, and harnessing that cultural and historical strength to deal with today's problems. Since the days of Dr. King, no prominent black American had dared to stand apart from the civil rights groupthink and ask, "Where do we go from here?" (which was the title of King's last book). That self-imposed censorship shows in the stagnant pool of ideas from which we black people draw when looking for solutions. It shows in the tired arguments rehearsed from the same predictable ideological positions. It shows in the lack of energy, imagination, or vision among our most visible leaders and organizations.

Cosby, of course, did not get to talk about strategies for black progress. But someone needs to. We're so trapped in anachronistic arguments and intimidated by ideology that we have rendered our own history useless to us. Is it time to explore whether Dr. King and Malcolm X, so often portrayed as two sides of a debate over dealing with race, might today have some complementary strategy for getting black America to move forward in the twenty-first century. How about Booker T. Washington's ideology of black self-reliance and W.E.B. DuBois's call for the best educated black Americans to show the way for all black people? Is there common ground in their thinking when dealing with the problems holding black America from soaring today?

Cosby was right. We *are* facing a series of crises in the black community today. A century's worth of progress seems suddenly in peril. The lessons and values that carried an oppressed people from slavery to freedom seem in danger of being forgotten. Hard-won victories seem in danger of being squandered. There are villains in this story: politicians drunk on their own rhetoric and power; the purveyors of a sick and destructive strain in our popular culture; and our complacent and self-isolated academic community. But there is also hope. Because we have within our culture what we need to move forward. We have a history of brilliantly effective politicians, grassroots activists, world-class scholars, life-affirming artists, and determined, hands-on educators who have moved millions around the world. We have Oseola McCarty.

Cosby was right, but he only told a portion of the story. Within his remarks is a declaration of what glory lies in our past, and the truth about what is going wrong today. This book picks up the baton to continue the race.

THE LEADERSHIP GAP

THE STINGING DART AT THE center of this controversy targets new black leadership.

Critics often charge Bill Cosby, in his *Brown* anniversary speech, with beating up on an easy mark: poor black people. Wrong. The critics are the ones who veer off target. Cosby repeatedly aimed his fire at the leaders of today's popular black culture, which is often not just created by black artists, but marketed and managed by black executives. He was also talking about current black political leaders and, most of all, about the civil rights leaders who time and time again send the wrong message to poor black people desperately in need of direction as they try to find their way in a society where being black and poor remains a unique burden to bear.

Cosby's point is that lost, poor black people have suffered most from not having strong leaders. His charge is that these leaders—cultural and political—misinform, mismanage, and miseducate by refusing to articulate established truths about what it takes to get ahead: strong families, education, and hard work. Every American has reason to ask about the seeming absence of strong black leadership. Where is strong black leadership to speak hard truth to those looking for direction? Where are the black leaders who will make it plain and say it loud? Who will tell you that if you want to get a job you have to stay in school and spend more money on education than on disposable consumer goods? Where are the black leaders who are willing to stand tall and say that any black man who wants to be a success has to speak proper English? Isn't that obvious? It would be a bonus if anyone dared to say to teenagers hungering for authentic black identity that dressing like a convict, whose pants are hanging off his ass because the jail prison guards took away his belt, is not the way to rise up and be a success.

There's a reason it takes strong leadership to make these points. It takes a leader to articulate why success in a world that so dramatically devalues black people is a worthwhile goal. When young people—and older people—take on a spirit of rebellion in their clothes, language, music, and other forms of expression, they're only responding in a fairly rational way to a society that has first insulted and degraded them. It takes a real leader to look beyond the immediate emotional satisfaction—and even the academic justification—of throwing up a middle finger in the face of the oppressor, and see the bigger picture. It takes a leader to think through the consequences and outline a better path—even if it requires sacrifice in the short term, sacrifice that may include giving up the easy emotional satisfaction of ultimately pointless acts, unexamined gestures of rebellion that never rise to the level of true resistance or long-term revolution. But that kind of leadership is sorely lacking.

Why have black leaders spent the last twenty years talking about reparations for slavery as if it were a realistic goal deserving of time and attention from black people? Why is rhetoric from our current core of civil rights leaders fixated on white racism instead of on the growing power of black Americans, now at an astounding level by any historical measure, to determine their own destiny? Fifty years after *Brown*, much of the power to address the problems facing black people is in black hands. Here is Cosby at the very start of his famous speech:

"I heard a prizefight manager say to his fellow, who was losing badly, 'David, listen to me, it's not what he's doing to you. It's what you're not doing.'"

Black Americans, including the poor, spend a lot of time talking about the same self-defeating behaviors that are holding back too many black people. This is no secret. It's practically a joke. And black people are the first to shake their heads at the scandals and antics of the current crop of civil rights leaders who are busy with old-school appeals for handouts instead of making maximum use of the power black people have in this generation to determine their own success.

So how did we end up in this situation? Black leaders have always risen to the occasion in the past, and in far more desperate situations—why does the talent bench seem so thin today? One key here is that nearly forty years after Reverend King's death, the best black talent don't have civil rights leadership as their chief ambition. Strong black intellects and personalities are leaders in media (Richard Parsons, the head of Time Warner, and Mark Whitaker, editor of *Newsweek*), securities firms (such as Stanley O'Neal of Merrill Lynch), global corporations (Kenneth Chenault of American Express, Ann Fudge of the public relations firm Young and Rubicam), academic institutions (Ruth Simmons, Kurt Schmoke, Henry Louis Gates, Ben Carson), religious organizations (Floyd Flake, T. D. Jakes), and national politics (Eleanor Holmes Norton, Artur Davis, Barack Obama, and Colin Powell).

That leaves the civil rights leadership of today in older hands: the Jesse Jacksons and Julian Bonds, people who made a name for themselves in the 1960s. And they are still fighting the battles of the 1960s. Then there are the latecomers, such as Al Sharpton, whose contribution is to mimic the aging leaders. Neither the old-timers nor their pale imitators recognize that national politics has changed and black people have changed. Hell, white people, as well as Hispanics, Asians, and other immigrants, have changed. Yet the black leadership is fighting the old battles and sending the same signals even as poor black people are stuck in a rut and falling further behind in a global economy.

Note that Cosby never identified himself as a civil rights leader. As he later put it, he is not Martin Luther King Jr. Cosby is a legendary figure in America's entertainment industry. He is at the top of his field. In speaking out, he presents himself as an ordinary man with a deep passion for the well-being of his people, black people. He is full of the rage of an average man who sees vulnerable people being hurt and feels compelled to speak out about the glaring errors and lack of truth-telling in dealing with their problems.

"I am not Jesus carrying a cross down the street," he told a reporter less than a month after the speech set fire to the controversy. "I gave the message and I may speak again and again. They want someone to do the work for them. I am not Dr. King. I am not a leader." But Cosby, like everybody else who is paying attention, recognizes bad leadership when he sees it.

One of Cosby's sharpest darts thrown at the current civil rights leaders hit home a few months after his Constitution Hall speech. He was at a town-hall meeting in Detroit to speak directly to black Americans in one of the nation's blackest cities. He wanted ordinary black people to hear from him directly about his comments at the *Brown* anniversary gala. When he reflected on today's black civil rights leaders, Cosby essentially asked, Why are black leaders making the case for black crack addicts to get softer sentences? Why are black leaders so concerned that cocaine users get shorter sentences than crack smokers? Let's look at the logic. It is true that the people snorting cocaine are more often white and middle-class, and crack addicts are disproportionately black and lower-class. You can make the case for a racial disparity in sentencing. But what if all this effort from black leaders was successful and crack addicts got lower sentences?

"Hooray," Cosby said, spitting it out bitterly. "Anybody see any sense in this? Systemic racism, they [black leaders] call it." Then Cosby pointed out the obvious issue—but one that the black civil rights leadership somehow missed or for some reason underplayed. Black leaders, he declared, should tell poor black people to stop smoking crack. They ought to demonize anybody who does it. They should say it is a betrayal of all the black people who fought to be free, independent, and in control of their own lives since the day the first slave ship landed. They should identify the crack trade as one of the primary reasons why so many young black people are ending up in jail. Certainly, back leaders should be in front of marches pushing those crack dealers out of black neighborhoods. And that effort should include a message that has yet to be heard with sincerity from black leaders: using crack, heroin, or any other addictive drug, including excessive drinking of alcohol, is self-destructive, breaks up families, saps ambition, and is more dangerous than most white racists.

But when was the last time you heard any civil rights leader raging against the clear evil of crack dealers, shaming them to stop selling crack? Has anyone seen the civil rights leaders at the head of a march against bad schools or a boycott against the

minstrel acts and sex, beer, and gangster images that are promoted as authentic black identity on Black Entertainment Television? *Essence*, a black women's magazine, has taken the lead in
condemning hateful verbal attacks on black women by black rap
musicians. But the most visible black leadership is silent.

The good news about black leadership in America is that it
has a history of inspirational success. Working against tremendous odds, black leaders have organized, built coalitions, and
trained and inspired people of all colors to break through racism,
taboos, and stereotypes to create the greatest social movement in
American history—the twentieth-century civil rights movement.

That movement offers examples and tools of consistently in-
novative leadership that have left America's political, corporate,
and cultural leaders hurrying to catch up. Movements for the
rights of women, Hispanics, children, and gays have all credited
the historical civil rights movement with opening doors for them,
and have made the black rights movement the model for achieving their own aspirations.

And that history of strong leadership offers an example of what
is possible for people who want to offer sincere, progressive leadership to black America today. Civil rights leaders have a fabulous
record of progress, excellence, and achievement, and a willingness
to fight and sacrifice for the next generation. Their commitment
to democracy, law, and equality has made the civil rights movement the moral center of America for the past century.

Even black leaders who lost battles along the way became legends by setting out a clear path of courageous struggle. Failure
wasn't desired, of course, but was willingly risked in the name of
standing up for what was right. From the start of slavery in the
United States, black leaders devised escapes, sabotaged plantation
operations, and plotted strategic acts of violence to defy the sys-

tem of human ruination that is slavery. Denmark Vesey led a slave revolt in 1822, in which he organized about 10,000 black people in both rural and urban areas around Charleston, South Carolina. At a time when black people outnumbered whites in the region, Vesey used black servants to spy on whites. He obtained and stored weapons, devised signals for his leaders to communicate, and had a clear plan for seizing the large arsenal in Charleston's harbor and using it to command the region. He recognized the power of religion and religious leaders in the black community, and used the church as a strategic center to identify leaders as well as recruit followers and hold meetings.

Ultimately the plot was uncovered and Vesey was hanged. But he ably demonstrated to black and white people the power of black people to throw off their identity as slaves and take on the mantle of self-determination as smart, courageous people in search of freedom. Less than ten years later, Nat Turner led a slave revolt of similar inspiration. These men were in a desperate situation, but these were not symbolic acts of self-destruction—they were organized resistance to an untenable status quo, and even in failure they inspired others to keep fighting and resisting.

Examples of the power of black leadership are evident in American history as early as 1780, when black leaders formed political groups to advance the right of black people to self-determination. The African Union Society of Newport for the Moral Improvement of Free Africans set requirements for the personal conduct of members who paid monthly dues for disability benefits and to be assured of proper burial. But the Union was also a political organization. It gave black people a voice in the city's political affairs with the goal of protecting equal rights for black people. The prize of black leadership, from that start, was always to have black people control their destiny by being able to educate their children, operate businesses, participate in politics as equals, and in the earliest struggle of all, live free of the exploitation of slave masters.

A streak of self-determination rises at every turn in the history of black American leadership. But since the stunning success of the modern civil rights movement—the steady rise since the *Brown* decision in the number of college-educated black people, as well as the concurrent growth in incomes, home ownership, and black elected officials—the strong focus on self-determination has faded, at the moment when its impact could have been the most powerful. In its place is a tired rant by civil rights leaders about the power of white people—what white people have done wrong, what white people didn't do, and what white people should do. This rant puts black people in the role of hapless victims waiting for only one thing—white guilt to bail them out.

The roots of this blacks-as-beggars approach from black leaders are planted in an old debate that is now too often distorted.

The most prominent voice for black liberation before the Civil War belonged to Frederick Douglass, a former slave who secretly taught himself how to read, then became a skilled worker in Baltimore's shipyards, before escaping to the freedom of the North. As a speaker, as the author of a book about his life in slavery, and as editor of a newspaper, the *North Star,* Douglass led the charge for all good people to stand against the abomination of slavery, including a call for black people to take up their own fight as a capable, strong force in American life. Douglass was the main black leader who pressed President Lincoln to allow black people to fight with the Union forces in the name of freeing themselves from slavery. All he asked of President Lincoln was that he officially emancipate the slaves so they could legally fight for their freedom. He personally recruited blacks, including his own two sons, for two regiments in Massachusetts. He asked the president for a military commission so he could lead black people in the fight for their own freedom. With Douglass pushing black people to be their own liberators, more than 200,000 black men put on the blue uniform of the Union. Once the war ended, he cited the black blood shed as the basis to call for black people to be given the right to vote and become full and equal members of the American family. And to freed slaves he also insisted on self-determination, telling them, "We need mechanics as well as ministers. We must build as well as live in houses; we must make as well as use furniture; we must construct bridges as well as pass over them." It was Douglass who first called on black people to do for themselves when he wrote an editorial titled "Learn Trades or Starve."

Douglass hammered this self-determinist ideology deep into the black American mind. By the end of the nineteenth century, as the government's many promises to help former slaves turned out to be mostly empty words, a new black leader emerged. Booker T. Washington picked up on Douglass's legacy by proposing defiant black self-determination as the best strategy for black advancement.

Washington wanted to build an economically powerful and independent black nation within the United States. He insisted that blacks command the respect of white citizens by virtue of independent black schools and black businesses. In seven years, between 1881 and 1888, Washington, another former slave, built the "Tuskegee Machine" in Alabama. He created a center of black education and economic activity to bring to life his vision of "black uplift."

The basis of Washington's strategy at Tuskegee had direct links to Douglass's theory of black self-reliance. His idea was that black people should capitalize on the skills and knowledge they had gained as slaves. People who had worked the land for others now had the chance to own that land and take the profits of their work for themselves. He had a vision of slaves using their work experience on plantations—as carpenters, plumbers, blacksmiths, veterinarians, maids, cooks, and morticians—to build a successful free black economy. He created "wagon schools on wheels" to teach the most efficient farming techniques to black farmers who could not come to the school. He planned for black people to pool their money by pursuing a "Gospel of Wealth," to buy the land they once worked as slaves. Washington's plan also included educating freed slaves and their children. He created a teaching staff of the best black craftsmen and farmers around the rural South. He saw them passing along their knowledge and building a base of economic strength for black America. Though Washington sought financial support from white patrons, his strategy was aimed at making black people economically self-sufficient. Writing in *The Atlantic Monthly* in 1896, Washington explained his plan:

> We find that as every year we put into southern community colored men who can start a brickyard, a sawmill, a tin shop, or a printing office, men who produce something that makes the white man partly dependent upon the Negro, instead of all the dependence being on the other side, a change takes place in race relations. Let us go on for a few more years knitting our business and industrial relations into those of the white man, till a black man gets a mortgage on a white man's house that he can foreclose at will. The white man on whose house that mortgage rests will not try to prevent that Negro from voting when he goes to the polls. . . . Whether he will or not, a white man respects a Negro who owns a two-story brick house.

Unlike Douglass, Washington felt that the best approach to advancing black power in American life was to carefully time and navigate his moves according to shifts in the opinions and personalities that determined national politics. He concluded that in a nation still struggling to unite after the Civil War, and where the South remained in economic turmoil, fierce demands by black people for equal political power as a civil right was not a winning hand. Playing to the bruised egos of defeated Southern whites, Washington was willing to forgo political activism and its focus on expanding black rights in exchange for being free to build black economic strength and self-reliance. "We should not permit our grievances to overshadow our opportunities," he said. That aspect of his plan struck some other black leaders as appeasement of resentful whites who fueled the Reconstruction era's violent attempt to reverse efforts to give blacks equal rights after the Civil War. He was seen as accepting racial segregation so as not to upset white racists. Similarly, his heavy focus on teaching black people how to work with their hands, as opposed to studying the liberal arts, led critics to charge him with lack of appreciation for the need to create black thinkers as a base for the next generation of black leaders.

This is the heart of a sincere ideological split about how best to advance the interests of black people as they strive for greater power. There was no disagreement between Douglass and Washington on the importance of black self-reliance and independence as the key to black progress. But there were some clear differences in their tactics and language.

At the time of Washington's rise, Douglass's influence was in decline. There was no black leader who compared to Washington in the reach of his influence and contacts in the world of white philanthropy and politics. But W.E.B. DuBois, the writer and political activist, stood tall enough as a social critic to offer a different point of view. And it is DuBois's respectful criticism of Washington that misled some black leaders to this day to lose sight of the mainstream of agreement in the foundational black leadership tradition. That devotion to self-determination was established by Douglass, Washington, and DuBois.

In fact they stood shoulder to shoulder in their belief that the best solution to America's race problem was for black people to stand tall and help themselves as equals in American life. Even at the height of their strategic disagreement at the start of the twentieth century, both DuBois and Washington had as their goal a prosperous black America, able to educate its children and establish strong businesses, as central to winning equal rights and full participation with whites in national life. DuBois found Washington a difficult personality, an autocrat, in that his "Tuskegee Machine" controlled political appointments, newspapers, and money from major foundations. Washington excluded independent thinkers like DuBois from his operations. But DuBois, in later writing about Washington, gave him credit by accurately describing him as "the greatest Negro leader since Frederick Douglass and the most distinguished man, white or black, who has come out of the south since the Civil War."

The key question for black leaders of the post–Civil War era was how to strengthen black people, then recently removed from slavery, so they could assert themselves as a power. Washington believed in compromise, favoring an approach that allowed for blacks and whites to be socially segregated but come together for mutual progress, all of which struck DuBois as lacking a willingness to express black "manhood." He saw Washington's ideas as "adjustment and submission" to white fears in the areas of political power, civil rights, and higher education in service to black economic progress. The heart of DuBois's differences with Washington came down to separate views on how to relate to the white majority as black people sought self-determination. But both saw whites as playing a role in helping people who had been denied equal rights in every area of life from education to political power for hundreds of years. DuBois, in his book *The Souls of Black Folk*, wrote that "while it is a great truth to say that the Negro must strive and strive mightily to help himself, it is equally true that unless his striving be not simply seconded but rather aroused and encouraged by . . . [the white majority] he cannot hope for great success." DuBois added that the burden of lifting former slaves to equal status in American life belonged to the whole "nation."

Having explained his differences with Washington, DuBois then stated his points of agreement with Washington, points of mutual goals that were too often overlooked. "So far as Mr. Washington preaches Thrift, Patience and Industrial Training for the masses, we must hold up his hands and strive with him."

This acknowledgment of a common goal of black self-reliance and power, the treasured prize of black political leadership, has been forgotten by black leaders at the start of the twenty-first century.

DuBois consistently saluted Washington for his efforts to strengthen black Americans as independent, prosperous people able to take their place at any political table as economic equals, as opposed to relying on their former status as slaves to beg for help. This desire for a sustainable, independent economic and cultural base was an unswerving, consistent message from black leaders of that era, ranging from Douglass to Washington to DuBois.

In fact, the biggest political movements of black people, before the *Brown* decision sparked the civil rights movement of the 1950s and 1960s, had self-determination as their hallmarks. Marcus Garvey's Negro Improvement Association, with its call for black economic power, worship of a black God, and even a return to Africa to be free of oppression, was an effort to move away from white domination and allow black people to take control of their lives. The Niagara Movement, which led to the creation of the NAACP, focused on strategies for defeating white political control of black people so that blacks could be free to determine their own future. A. Philip Randolph, who brought black workers into the American labor movement with his Brotherhood of Sleeping Car Porters, also stressed the power of black people to organize so they could determine their own interests and create a base for building alliances with white workers. Randolph used the power of organized black labor to press President Roosevelt to integrate the industries supplying the war effort; he threatened a black march on Washington in 1941 to force the president to end discrimination against black workers. "Power is the flower of organization," Randolph said. And the organization he led was one in which black people came together to fight for equal rights as workers and citizens.

The *Brown* decision itself is an example of black American leadership focused on self-determination, in this case the right to get an equal share of tax dollars to educate their children. A deliberate strategy of attacking segregation in graduate and professional schools led to the challenge against segregation in elementary and secondary schools and the victory in *Brown*. The NAACP had its name on the cases, but wasn't alone in this struggle: black organizations ranging from fraternal groups to church groups and social clubs organized with a clear purpose of supporting more independence for black people to properly educate their children.

The Montgomery Bus Boycott, featuring Rosa Parks's famous refusal to move to the back of the bus, is another example of black people organizing for self-determination. Parks was a member of a group, the Women's Political Council, that had been working against segregation on the bus lines for months before Parks was arrested. In fact, the group inspired Parks by raising her awareness of the oppressive control of racism that extended to the daily insult of Parks and every other black person in Montgomery being told where to sit on a bus. The all-black council, led by a black college professor, Jo Ann Robinson, brought together black and white women to fight against segregation on the buses. One of the women was Rosa Parks. And when she was arrested she reached out to Robinson and the women in the group for support. That led black ministers to join in the effort, including twenty-five-year-old Martin Luther King Jr. of the Dexter Avenue Baptist Church. And with Robinson, King, and others holding fast, the black community in the Alabama capital organized transportation to get themselves around town while they boycotted the white-run buses for an entire year. It was a classic case of black self-determination, and it ended with a Supreme Court victory over racial discrimination in local public transit that increased the rights of all black Americans.

Black pride in taking control of their own fate was a defiant rejection of the image of blacks as victims, ignorant, and lazy. It was driven by a raw faith in the power of black people to compete and thrive in a democratic, capitalistic nation if given the chance to be equals. And if the chance wasn't given, then it was taken, by whatever means were appropriate and effective, from organizing to direct protest to legal battles. This is what unified black leadership and organizations over a century of struggle: even when there were differences in tactics and philosophies, there was a unity of mission.

It's also often forgotten that, later in his life, DuBois's position on the critical importance of building a sustainable black economy bore some resemblance to the ideas of the Wizard of Tuskegee. Their rivalry was real—as were the stakes—but is no longer relevant. The areas where these two great men agreed are of more interest to us today. They both stood, in the end, for black self-help and dignity—and, ultimately, for full citizenship rights. Their priorities were different and so were their tactics, but their ultimate goals were more or less the same. They both gave their lives to that goal.

Today, some look back at that history through a different lens, arguing about which side to stand with—Washington or DuBois— as if the two figures represented good and evil (or at least competing ideologies). This false choice—DuBois or Washington, protest or accommodation—became a preoccupation in setting leadership styles as black Americans went through the civil rights movement and developed political power. Black radicals idolized DuBois and demonized Washington. Any strategy that included compromise was criticized as Booker T. Washington–style accommodation and appeasement. Martin Luther King Jr., with his record of achievement, was subject to being attacked for being too moderate and "unmanly" in attracting white financial support in the manner of Washington. The NAACP, which led the fight for the *Brown* decision, became a target for similar distrust and dismissal as younger people joined the movement and accused the Roy Wilkinses and Thurgood Marshalls of the world of moving too slowly, and being too close to the white establishment.

The tragedy was that this infighting managed to diminish attention to a bright and bold fact of history: Black leaders of all ideological stripes agreed that the key to racial progress was black people helping themselves. King, for example, said he wanted above all else to get black people to shed the idea that they did not control their destiny, an idea he attributed to the power of racists to infect black people with self-defeating doubts about inferiority and create a psychological need to rely on whites for their well-being. Speaking about the victories of the 1960s civil rights era, King said, "The real victory was what this period did to the psyche of the black man. . . . We armed ourselves with dignity and self-respect. The greatness of this period was that we straightened our backs up. And a man can't ride your back unless it's bent."

King's belief in black self-determination was evident throughout his career. In 1960, before the success of the March on Washington and the passage of civil rights laws, he told an Urban League conference that "if first-class citizenship is to become a reality for the Negro, he must assume primary responsibility for making it so. The Negro must not be victimized with the delusion of thinking that others should be more concerned than himself about his citizenship rights." Today, King's words apply to black Americans taking advantage of opportunities that did not exist a generation ago.

After the past twenty years of stagnation in the civil rights movement, Cosby's words have entered public discussion like a gust of fresh air. And they come at a moment when the nation is facing global challenges including terrorism and competition from emerging economic powers. Skilled high-technology workers are now being produced in China, India, and Eastern Europe. They are taking jobs in the new economy and leaving black Americans who lack good educations farther behind. Meanwhile, low-income jobs in textiles and manufacturing are not only leaving the United States, but an unprecedented wave of immigrants is arriving and taking service industry jobs, as cleaning staff, waiters, and gardeners.

The civil rights leadership's focus on replaying battles with whites of the 1950s and 1960s is totally out of touch with the present global challenge, which demands an emphasis on aggressively taking advantage of opportunities for education, training, entrepreneurship, and investment. Now that the doors are open to global competition, no one is giving away opportunities anymore. If people in power didn't want to cede opportunity to African Americans when their own positions were secure, they certainly don't want to do so now that their place at the top of the economic ladder is threatened by a wide-open field of competition from around the world. Beyond jobs, that includes competition to get into school, and competition inside the classroom. The clear fact is that even in the field of education, affirmative action is not long for the United States. Justice Sandra Day O'Connor, in writing a Supreme Court opinion allowing the University of Michigan to use race as a factor in selecting students, said plainly that affirmative action has twenty-five years remaining, at most, as a tool of social policy in the United States—and this before her place on the court was assumed by an even more conservative justice. Affirmative action in business is also under attack, and its cause is weakened all too often by highly publicized charges of corruption whenever black figureheads are placed atop white companies for the purpose of gaming the system, allowing white-owned firms to win contracts intended as set-asides for minorities.

Frederick Douglass, Booker T. Washington, and W.E.B. DuBois all agreed that black people had to strive for opportunity and grab it by the throat. In their minds, anyone who didn't advance that idea was no friend of the black man in America—and the same is true today. And anyone—including black leaders—who confuses black people about what it takes for their children to make progress is no friend. Over the last decades, black Americans have benefited from court decisions like *Brown v. Board of Education*, the civil rights laws that offered some political legal protection, and the development of strong political voices to advocate civil rights positions. But these things can only take black America so far. At some point, people have to take a personal accounting, turn away from any self-defeating behavior, and be sure they are doing everything in their power to put their families and their communities in a position to prosper and advance.

Cosby's pointed reminder that in the fifty years after *Brown*, black people, especially poor black people, are not "holding up their end of the deal" by taking advantage of new opportunities to stand tall, is the message that father figures such as Douglass, Washington, and DuBois delivered in their time. It is the current version of Douglass's editorial, "Learn Trades or Starve." This is the core message of black leadership in American history. It is the sin of this generation of leadership that it has lost track of black America's most valuable truth, and has failed to speak that truth to poor black people looking for the light of the Promised Land. As the Christian faith teaches, "God helps those who help themselves."

2

BLOOD OF THE MARTYRS AND OTHER BAD EXCUSES

FIFTY YEARS AFTER THE *Brown* decision, President George W. Bush made a controversial speech about black people, too.

Caught up in a political fight with the NAACP since the 2000 presidential campaign, the president shunned the group's 2004 summer meeting and chose to speak to the annual Urban League convention instead. The Republican George W. Bush, who got only 8 percent of the black vote in the 2000 race, used the speech to present a challenge to black America: Why should more than 90 percent of black people vote for the Democrat in presidential elections, he asked, when the worst schools in the nation are big-city schools for black and Hispanic students?

It was a good question. How is it possible that under Democratic mayors and governors, unions loyal to the Democratic Party, and decades of Democratic control of Congress, the schools have continued to fail minority children? Big-city schools have become increasingly segregated by race and class in the last thirty years. Their academic performance has declined. In addition, the black middle class has joined whites in moving out to the suburbs to get their children away from those schools. The black poor, in defiance of black politicians, have told pollsters they favored vouchers, charter schools, and magnet schools to give them some chance to get their children out of those bad public schools, too.

"Progress for African Americans and progress for all Americans requires good schools," the president said. "Look, the system tended to shuffle kids through. And you know what I'm talking about. You know, the hard-to-educate were labeled . . . and moved through. That's what was happening. We can play like it wasn't happening—it was happening . . . it's what I call the soft bigotry of low expectations."

President Bush pointed out that his administration was working to improve schools and close the "achievement gap" between black and white students by demanding that schools be held accountable if children can't read, write, and do math. He asked for the black vote and said he wanted to earn it by giving black children a better chance to get a high school and college education. He said he had increased funding for Pell Grants and for historically black colleges. And he added that he took pride in having named the first black secretary of education, Rod Paige. He had two simple questions for black voters: What had Democrats done to earn their vote? And does the Democratic Party take the black vote for granted?

"Is it a good thing for the African American community to be represented mainly by one political party?" the president asked at the Urban League convention. "It's a legitimate question. How is it possible to gain political leverage if the party is never forced to compete?"

The questions went unanswered until Al Sharpton stood up a month later at the 2004 Democratic convention in Boston. As a candidate who ran for the party's nomination, Sharpton was given the chance to speak in prime time before a national audience. Three sentences into his speech, Sharpton said he'd attended the president's Urban League speech, and "I would like to answer your questions, Mr. President."

An ordained preacher since he was twelve and a brilliant orator, the ever-flamboyant Sharpton responded that fifty years after the *Brown* decision, quality education for all children is at the heart of what he called "the promise of America." But he moved past that issue to delight the audience with an allegorical reference to the donkey that is the symbol of the Democratic Party. He said blacks had ridden that mule to get the Voting Rights Act and the Civil Rights Act, and he said it had been Democrats—under President Johnson—who, like a donkey, stubbornly stood by blacks when civil rights workers were killed in Mississippi and the movement's leader, Martin Luther King Jr., was assassinated.

"Mr. President, you [asked], 'Would we have more leverage if both parties got our votes?' But we didn't come this far playing political games. It was those who earned our votes who got our votes. . . . Our vote was soaked in the blood of martyrs, soaked in the blood of Goodman, Chaney, and Schwerner, soaked in the blood of four little girls in Birmingham. This vote is sacred to us. This vote can't be bargained away . . . given away. Mr. President, in all due respect, read my lips: Our vote is not for sale!"

The crowd roared.

Roared for what?

Where was the substance about steps being taken by Democrats to give black children better schools? How had the party put itself on the line to help halt the shockingly high rate of black children born into poverty as a result of being born to single mothers? What record did the Democrats have on dealing with the maddening number of young black people in the grip of the cancerous prison system?

The answer: absolutely nothing. But by waving the red flag labeled "blood of martyrs," Sharpton diverted all attention from dealing with bad schools, persistent high rates of unemployment, and a range of issues that are crippling a generation of black youth. Somehow, "blood of martyrs" remains the anthem of black politics at the start of the twenty-first century. Black politics is still defined by events that took place forty years ago. Protest marches are reenacted again and again as symbolic exercises to the point that they have lost their power to achieve change. As a result, black politics is paralyzed, locked in synchronized salute and tribute, by any mention of the martyrs, the civil rights workers who died violent deaths at the hands of racists. The major national black politicians invoke these icons and perform shallow reenactments of the powerful marches of the movement as hypnotic devices to control their audiences. And if people try to break the spell by suggesting we move beyond those ancient heroes and tired tactics, they are put down with language that implicates them as tools of the white establishment, reactionaries who've "forgotten their roots." Race traitors.

So far, the "blood of martyrs" strategy has had tragic results for the progress of poor black people, but it has worked magnificently for a few national black politicians. Prominent leaders like Al Sharpton and Jesse Jackson, neither of whom has ever won an election or held political office, have—through the force of their personalities and rhetoric, and the limitations of their ideas and strategies—slowed the emergence of any new model of national black political leadership. Very few new ideas are allowed into this stifling echo chamber. Late-twentieth-century black politics grew out of a youthful, vibrant civil rights movement. But today national black politics is dry and dusty with age.

Jackson's claim to black leadership was to make a show of literally having Dr. King's blood on him after the 1968 assassination.

The day after King's death, he went on TV in a shirt that he said was covered with King's blood. Jackson was able to raise money and start his own civil rights organization by advertising himself to the white media as the new King. And he made an art of protests and boycotts against big companies that refused to make concessions to him in the name of racial justice. He demanded the hiring of black executives as well as black workers. He called for corporations to do business with black-owned firms, and to make contributions to his group. Many of the black firms that got business as a result of Jackson's efforts also made contributions to Jackson's group, PUSH. One of Jackson's big supporters in the black community was Bill Cosby. The comedian made large contributions to Jackson's group and put on free performances to boost Jackson and his organization. Cosby delighted in Jackson's ability to debate top white political leaders, and was inspired by his talent as a speaker and his daring in traveling overseas to bring home American hostages.

In 1984, Jackson used his status as heir to King to run for president and establish himself as the nation's leading black politician. He ran again in 1988 and got more votes than he had the first time, finishing with the second-highest delegate total in the Democratic primaries. But he never came close to winning the nomination—and it's safe to say that he never had any expectation, or perhaps even any intention, of actually winning the nomination. Jackson ran as a civil rights crusader, using the platform of a national political campaign to raise issues of racial injustice. His real achievement turned out to be bulldozing the rapidly increasing number of grassroots community leaders, local black politicians, members of congress, mayors, and even a governor—Douglas Wilder of Virginia. During and after his presidential runs, he traveled into cities and marginalized local black politicians with his pop-star news coverage, forcing them into his shadow. The media loved the story of the first major campaign by a black candidate for his party's presidential nomination. Jackson's ties to Dr. King and the threat that he might be attacked or killed made the story all the more irresistible. When the Nation of Islam's leader, Louis Farrakhan, pledged to protect Jackson's life after Jackson called New York "Hymie town" (a disparaging reference to the city's large Jewish population), the media coverage, even while turning negative, became even more feverish.

Jackson got an enthusiastic response from black voters and white liberals with his defiance of Ronald Reagan's supply-side economics and tax cuts for the rich. His denunciation of the Republican's attacks on affirmative action got a fervently positive response from black voters. Jackson—with the novelty of his race, his authentically inspiring oratory, and his populist agenda—generated excited news coverage, especially as compared with Mondale and Dukakis, the two lackluster white Democrats he ran against. Even as he was losing the race, he was clearly the star on the Democratic campaign trail. Large audiences, black and white, turned out to see him. Jackson was confirmed as the preeminent black leader of his time.

Ultimately, Jackson's two campaigns ended with the same question: "What Does Jesse Want?" As the kingpin of the black vote, the core of the Democrats' base in American politics, he held the key to high levels of black turnout. What concessions did Jackson want from the party's presidential candidates, Walter Mondale in 1984 and Michael Dukakis in 1988? Both Mondale and Dukakis easily outpaced him in getting votes and winning the nomination, but they needed black voters in the general election. So what would it take to get him to fire up the black base for the Democrats' candidates? Using the model he had put in place to wring concessions from corporate America during his days as the leader of Operation PUSH, Jackson made demands of the nominees. Of course, this is also the nature of American politics: a candidate who can legitimately claim to represent a constituency is supposed to leverage that claim to make demands on behalf of that constituency. Here's what Jackson demanded: He wanted control of some jobs on the general election campaign staff and control of contracts in black media for get-out-the-vote efforts among black voters. He also wanted an airplane for his use during the general election, and he wanted to be paid for his efforts. In the end, Jackson increased black voter turnout in 1984, but Mondale lost in a landslide to Ronald Reagan. And while he got more votes in 1988, Jackson did not increase black voter registration or turnout in the general election.

The net political result from the two campaigns was that Jackson, in the eyes of many black voters, but even more so in the eyes of the white media and political establishment, became the unofficial president of black America. But in terms of winning and losing the White House, the bottom line was that Jackson's candidacy was used by Republicans to add momentum to their drive to get Northern white ethnics to leave behind their tradition of voting for Democrats since the days of Franklin Delano Roosevelt, as well as their loyalty to unions allied with Democrats. He was a key to the emergence of "Reagan Democrats." In the south, Jackson's candidacy was used to speed the development of complete Republican domination by pushing white males into the GOP. Although it certainly wasn't his fault that the backlash against his success only crippled his party's ability to enact any of his agenda, the fact is that his candidacy was a plus for Jackson personally and a plus for Republicans, but did very little in practical terms for the very people he claimed to represent. Just as Jackson's campaign was never about winning the nomination, neither was it about actually affecting progress on any of the key political issues affecting life for black people, from bad schools to unemployment. Nevertheless, long after the 1988 presidential campaign, Jackson remained the face of national black politics, able to get media attention for his comments and response to issues facing black people. Jesse Jackson held a mythical post—President of Black America. On any issue affecting black America, the media's one-stop shopping for a comment was Jesse Jackson.

When offered the chance to hold a real political post with the power to put into action new policies for helping black people, the poor, and the oppressed, Jackson said no. He turned away from political races he had a chance to win by refusing to run for mayor in Chicago, the hometown of his group PUSH, or to run for the U.S. Senate from South Carolina, his native state. As a result, he was not involved in passing any new laws to improve schools, reduce health problems in the black community, or any other key issue facing black America. And he was not accountable to any constituency for his lack of progress. He did enrich his family. He got the country's top beer company, Budweiser, which he'd boycotted in the 1980s with the slogan "Bud's a Dud," to sell a multimillion-dollar beer distribution center to two of his sons. But despite his lack of actual political achievement, Jackson remained the kingpin of black politics.

When Jackson was caught in a scandal over having a child with one of his aides, Al Sharpton began an aggressive push to succeed Jackson as the President of Black America. His call for a new generation of leadership was based on his ability to fill Jackson's rhetorical role, speaking words of outrage over racism and attracting media coverage of any incident in which blacks appeared to be victimized by whites. But when Sharpton ran for president in

2004, he did not win a single primary. He didn't even come close to winning in New York City, where he is best known. And he didn't win in South Carolina, where blacks make up most of the Democratic primary voters. He got far fewer votes and convention delegates than Jackson did. He got fewer delegates than New York City Congresswoman Shirley Chisholm did when she ran a purely symbolic campaign as the first black candidate for a party's presidential nomination in 1972.

Sharpton did take the Jackson model of modern black politics to a new low, however. To finance his failing campaign, he reportedly took about $200,000 from a Republican political strategist known for playing dirty politics, Roger Stone. The only time Stone showed an interest in black politics was when he joined the effort to block a recount of black and Jewish votes in Miami-Dade County to protect candidate George W. Bush's presidential victory in the 2000 election. In 2004 he joined hands with Sharpton and eventually placed one of his top aides in control of Sharpton's campaign. As reporter Mark Bowden later wrote in *The Atlantic Monthly*, "There could be only one plausible reason for Stone's helping Sharpton and that was to undermine the mainstream appeal of the Democratic Party by forcing whoever became the front runner to deal with Sharpton's ostentatiously leftist agenda."

It also revealed a deep cynicism at the heart of national black politics. The Jackson model had the virtue of at least bringing issues of concern to black Americans onto the biggest political stage in American life—a presidential campaign—and stirring black political pride and interest in national politics. Sharpton, by contrast, was running a campaign solely about his own personal ambition to get on the national stage, even to the point of working as a mole inside the Democratic primary for the Republican Party.

This wasn't the first time Sharpton had taken on that role. In 1988, New York *Newsday* reported that Sharpton had secretly given federal agents information on black leaders in New York City. The newspaper claimed that Sharpton had worked privately for the FBI after he had been videotaped in 1983 apparently asking about buying cocaine from an undercover FBI agent. As recently as 2005, Sharpton took money from a company called LoanMax in exchange for appearing in ads designed to lure poor black people into their financial web. The company offered to loan money at high interest rates to poor people with bad credit histories if they agreed to put up the titles to their cars as collateral. Similar car-title lenders had demanded interest rates of up to 300 percent, a level of usury that resulted in high profits for the lenders, especially when poor people defaulted on their loans and lost their cars. This kind of exploitation of the vulnerable is why about half of the states ban such loans. *The New Republic* concluded that the incident was proof that Sharpton's "professed concern for the poor and downtrodden is an obvious charade."

The real meaning of Sharpton- and Jackson-style politics can best be seen away from the spotlight of a presidential contest. In the shadowy world of corporate public relations, where charges of racism in dealing with customers, hiring, and contracting can do major damage to a brand, Jackson and Sharpton have created an industry.

One particularly ugly example came to light when Sharpton took money from one white-owned company that wanted to force another white-owned firm, a cable television company named Charter Communications, to carry their programming. Having failed to negotiate a deal with Charter, Detroit firm Adell Broadcasting Corporation hired Sharpton to stage a phony civil rights protest march in front of Charter Communications' offices.

Sharpton got out of a limousine in March 2002, according to reporting in the *Wall Street Journal*, to lead three busloads of protest
marchers in chants of "No Justice, No Peace," outside of Charter's headquarters near St. Louis. One of the protest organizers
working with Sharpton said he got people to join the protest by
pulling them out of homeless shelters, giving them a meal and
fifty dollars. He told the *Journal* that "I like to refer to it as a 'rent
a demonstration.'"

Sharpton took home a lot more than fifty dollars for his role
in the sham. The newspaper said his usual fee for leading a
demonstration that exploited the memory of civil rights era
demonstrations was at least $10,000. Jesse Jackson had also been
similarly paid by Adell Broadcasting to put racial pressure on
Charter. Jackson's response to the report was to say, "It is not unusual for the people that we help to help the organization. That
does not affect our integrity at all. It's the way we survive."

But survive to do what and serve what end?

Is the survival of organizations like Jackson's Operation PUSH
leading the nation to face up to the sin of not giving a good education to most black and Hispanic children? Is their survival forcing anyone to confront the high rates of young black men in jail?
Does money in Jackson's or Sharpton's pockets—or in the coffers
of their campaigns and organizations—help with the shockingly
low number of black people who have health insurance? When
Jackson and Sharpton attack the president of Mexico over a Sambo
image on a postage stamp, and get lots of time on the TV news,
does it really make a difference in the life of a single black person
in this country?

Jackson and Sharpton's explanation for staging phony protest
marches for money (as well as spending weeks railing against a
picture on a stamp in a foreign country) lacked credibility. Once
again, Jackson's rationale came into play—"It's the way we survive."

This base way of thinking has pulled the cause of civil rights far away from the moral high ground. How is anyone to tell the difference between Jackson and Sharpton at the head of a phony march or a real march?

Different streams of the midcentury Civil Rights Movement in this country advocated for different immediate goals and different ways, but they did have some things in common. Dr. King invoked God's name in appealing to the Judeo-Christian principles of conscience with his calls for racial equality and liberty for all. Thurgood Marshall and the NAACP Legal Defense Fund appealed to the ideals written in America's law, the Constitution, to insist on justice for all. Malcolm X decried the hypocrisy of a nation that called itself a democracy and yet allowed black people in the South to be beaten when they tried to vote. King, Marshall, and Malcolm X all made their appeals to transform the nation's soul and open opportunities for people regardless of race—not for themselves, their friends, or the highest corporate bidder. There was no smell of extortion in their movements.

Under Jackson and Sharpton, the high moral standing of civil rights has eroded, slid downhill, and now rests precariously on the rationale of "it's the way we survive." Even the once-august NAACP now plays softball politics. On the promise of easier access to money and power if Democrats hold power, the group tried to rally opposition to President Bush in the 2000 campaign. They used a TV commercial that made it appear that candidate Bush, while governor of Texas, had refused to punish two white men who had dragged a black man, James Byrd, to his death behind a truck in Jasper, Texas. The murder of Byrd was a horrific crime, a modern-day lynching, but the fact is that the perpetrators were given the maximum sentence. Then-governor Bush did refuse to sign legislation that might have added to their sentence by declaring the murder a "hate crime." But that was an argument over legislation—and the NAACP could have reasonably argued that Bush was wrong on that piece of legislation. But instead, the NAACP used that narrower argument to portray the governor as a member of the lynch mob. Their goal was to use deeply felt fears of racial violence to stir up black votes and get them to oppose Bush, to conjure the most horrific image from the African American past—the lynching—to eliminate all nuance from the debate among black voters about which presidential candidate could do a better job of solving problems in black America. The devious tactic worked: Bush, who got about a third of the black vote when he ran for governor in Texas, got only 8 percent of the national black vote in his 2000 presidential bid, a drop attributable at least in part to the opposition of the NAACP. The scare tactics made the NAACP an important player on the national political scene, but it burned up the higher moral ground that once was the basis of black politics.

And there were more scare tactics as Bush and Al Gore, his Democratic opponent, battled for more than a month over votes in Florida to determine the winner of the 2000 contest. Again, the NAACP, with Jackson and Sharpton also on board, incited fear that racist Republicans had denied black people the right to vote. They spoke with conviction of purges of voter registration lists in black neighborhoods, polling places being mysteriously moved, and the use of police to intimidate black voters. In fact, Florida Republicans did aggressively try to get felons off the voter registration rolls, especially if they lived in black areas. The Republicans clearly wanted to suppress black votes because they were votes for Democrats. And there were problems for people who registered to vote when they got their driver's licenses because the system, under a Republican secretary of state, didn't work well. But when the U.S. Justice Department, led by Democrats appointed by President Bill Clinton, investigated the charges they came up empty. There were anecdotes about GOP dirty tricks to scare off black voters. But the Justice Department found no basis for any charges of black people being denied the right to vote. Once again, the moral power of black politics was sacrificed.

NAACP Chairman Julian Bond followed up the damage done to black political power in 2000 with a vitriolic speech at the group's convention in July 2001. He damned the Republican president as a racist right-wing candidate. After noting that 60 percent of white men and a majority of white women voted for Bush, the NAACP chair said of the new president, then in office only five months, "He has selected nominees from the Taliban wing of American politics, appeased the wretched appetites of the extreme right wing, and chosen Cabinet officials whose devotion to the Confederacy is nearly canine in its uncritical affection."

Bond's assessment came at a time when the president had already named a black man as secretary of state. He had a Mexican-American as his White House counsel, Asian Americans as his transportation and labor secretaries, and a black woman as his national security advisor. One step below the cabinet level, the president had a black woman in charge of hiring for the government as head of the Office of Personnel Management, and a black man in charge of all government property as head of the General Services Administration. He also put a black man in charge of the Federal Communications Commission. That president also banned the use of racial profiling by federal law enforcement agents, and the civil rights division of the Justice Department agreed to reopen a probe into the infamous 1950s murder of a black teen in Mississippi, Emmett Till.

But to listen to Bond, it sounded as if the president were a racist white politician in the tradition of former Alabama governor George Wallace—the segregationist who played to racial hatred when he stood in the schoolhouse door to block black students from attending the state university. President Bush certainly has his shortcomings on racial policies, but there is no reality to any claim of the president regularly stirring white hatred of minorities. That didn't matter. The point for Bond was to make the president into a monster and scare the audience into racial solidarity and support for the NAACP.

In the same speech, Bond noted that because of the NAACP's success, "America tolerates much less discrimination today than in years past." He said it was a "lesson for our future," and evidence that black people "have succeeded against great odds in the past." Yet he made no mention of the most important fight of modern times—the battle to make good schools available to black children so they can compete in a fierce global economic market. He made no mention of strengthening black America by proposing plans to help black people make maximum use of scholarships, training programs, and loans for business development. He proposed no plan for cutting down high rates of HIV/AIDS and diabetes. There was no mention that black people had the power to change their sexual behavior or their diet to deal with these health problems. The idea of black power, black responsibility, and accountability—keys to black America's progress over centuries—was missing.

Bond's strategy allowed his political enemies in the Bush administration and the Republican Party to claim the moral high ground. With outreach efforts through black churches and black businesses, the GOP has put money into programs that effectively deal with the children of black prisoners and with drug addicts, and put in place an education plan to force big-city schools to do a better job with black children. Bond and the NAACP have responded with charges that whites cannot choose black leadership. Again, the response is to wave the bloody flag of old fights instead of looking for opportunities to advance the needs of black America.

The same cynical claim that "it's the way we survive" has roots in big-city politics. In the aftermath of the civil rights movement, black political power took control in many urban centers. Tom Bradley in Los Angeles, Harold Washington in Chicago, Maynard Jackson and Andrew Young in Atlanta, and David Dinkins in New York struggled mightily to govern cities with large populations of poor people and tax bases drained by white flight and suburban malls. Even with their cities on shaky financial ground, these black mayors focused on opening doors for black people to get goods and services from the city, and for black businesses to get a share of city contracts.

But another brand of black mayor emerged as well. Sharpe James in Newark and Marion Barry in Washington, D.C., ran entire city governments based on handing out jobs and contracts to their pals, and bullying anyone who challenged their hold on power by accusing them of undercutting black leadership and engaging in racism. These mayors operated in the worst tradition of big-city club politics, even to the point of breaking the law, which in Barry's case included being caught on videotape smoking crack. James allowed Newark's potential for growth, as New York's nearest neighbor, to be squandered in favor of maintaining his complete control over the city's treasury. Newark and Washington have the ingredients for attracting major corporations and a more-diverse residential population. But James and Barry saw political opportunity in making themselves masters of large pools of poor black people dependent on state and federal poverty programs. Both mayors led administrations that accepted high crime and failing schools as a way of life for poor black people. Any challenge to their dominion, any call for accountability, was portrayed by them as the tactics of whites trying to gain control of the city and undercut a black leader. The result was a total absence of accountability. Corruption scandals, high taxes, and poor delivery of city services became the hallmarks of these black governments. Any criticism was labeled as racist.

Both Barry and James saw scandals and allegations of mismanagement define their governments and scar the reputation of black politics. Top aides to both men were convicted on corruption charges.

Barry's campaign manager Ivanhoe Donaldson, like Barry a former civil rights activist with the Student Nonviolent Coordinating Committee (SNCC), pleaded guilty to stealing money from the city, including cash for the unemployed. He also used tax dollars to repair his Mercedes-Benz. The chair of Barry's inauguration was granted about 40 percent of the city's housing acquisition money during Barry's first term. The waiting list for public housing grew even as apartments remained vacant because Barry's administration failed to repair them. The school system hit highs in dropouts as reading scores hit new lows. The courts had to take control of the jails because of overcrowding. The city's minority set-aside contracting program was "rife" with corruption, according to auditors, and the beneficiaries were the mayor's friends. Under Barry the city government paid a real estate developer who contributed to Barry's campaigns—and was godfather to Barry's son—$11 million for land valued at $6.7 million. D.C. had the highest per-capita taxes for the top big cities in the nation, but used the revenues to pay for the largest city government payroll in the nation—a bloated workforce that owed its paycheck to the boss-man, the mayor.

In Newark, Mayor James's chief of staff, Jackie R. Mattison, was found guilty of taking bribes to give contracts to an insurance broker. His police chief was convicted of stealing money. The city's failing public school system was described as "patronage-ridden." The register of deeds pleaded guilty to taking kickbacks in return for handing out millions in contracts to repair public housing. Over three years more than a dozen top employees in the city's housing authority donated more than $22,000 to the mayor's reelection campaign. Meanwhile a federal audit found "widespread mismanagement" of low-income housing, including $6.4 million in "misspent" funds. During James's time in office, the city council also fell into corruption: two members were convicted of extortion, and a third pleaded guilty to extortion. Mayor James meanwhile attracted the attention of investigators by piling up millions in the Sharpe James Civic Association, a group that never registered as a charity or a political action committee. The fund was under the mayor's personal control, and it accepted money from people seeking contracts with the city. The mayor refused to account for how the money was spent. Much of it, according to bank statements, went into his reelection campaigns. But while in office, James managed to buy a $160,000 yacht, a $300,000 beach house, and five condominiums. The mayor was never convicted of any crime. When James won a close race for mayor in 2002, his star supporter on the campaign trail was Jesse Jackson.

Barry and James won reelection time and again. In both cities the mayors-for-life used fear of whites coming back to the city to repel any criticism of corruption and poor public services. They portrayed reformers, black and white, as stand-ins for the wealthy, powerful whites. Using the "blood of martyrs" rhetoric, they reminded black voters that, throughout history, powerful black leaders often faced white critics. "I'm not going to be lynched," Barry said during one corruption probe.

James and Barry also encouraged a perverse pride among powerless blacks in seeing a black man stay a step ahead of the law (in Barry's case, the law finally videotaped him smoking crack, so there was no question of his guilt). They also benefited from the "it's our turn" argument. European-American political bosses—Dutch, British, German, Irish, and Italian—had for decades dominated American big cities, often stooping to massive corruption and ignoring the needs of black people. So, to some observers, the spectacle of black politicians exploiting the poor residents they represent is no different from the exploitation of the other ethnic bosses who preceded them. It's simply "our turn." But the difference, of course, is that black political power is rooted in the ideals of the civil rights movement. The dream of black political power was about truly serving people, specifically repairing the damage of racist politics that neglected black neighborhoods and schools. The promise was to finally serve the needs of black people, providing them a fair shot at educating their children, getting good jobs, living in safe, healthy neighborhoods, and pulling themselves into economic security. Instead, their reigns were defined by Jackson's theme—"it's the way we survive."

That corrupt attitude reached into the nation's largest black church organization, the National Baptist Convention. Reverend Henry J. Lyons used his large following in the nation's black churches to enter into illegal deals with corporations that wanted to peddle funeral homes, cemetery plots, life insurance, credit cards, and more to black churchgoers. He was convicted of lying to those white-owned businesses about the size of his group's membership in order to get more than $4 million from them.

Prosecutors convicted him of racketeering and grand theft. He later pleaded guilty to bank fraud and tax evasion. Lyons was also found guilty of stealing nearly a quarter-million dollars that a Jewish group, the Anti-Defamation League of B'nai B'rith, had contributed to repair churches that had been damaged by an arsonist. And what did Lyons do with the money? Did he invest it in repairing black churches and improving schools? No, he used the money to buy jewelry, take lavish vacations, and purchase a $700,000 waterfront house for his mistress. That last extravagance led his wife to set fire to the house and attracted federal investigators.

It is what happened after Lyons's conviction, however, that really makes the story emblematic of the acceptance of a culture of political corruption among many black American leaders. Most of the leadership and members of the National Baptist Convention rallied to defend Lyons, a man who had lied and stolen from them. They cited corrupt white ministers, such as Jimmy Swaggart, to argue that church leaders of all colors had problems. They completely failed to consider the critical role the church played in black American life, and why it was such a betrayal of vulnerable people in need of honest leaders—poor and working-class black people who put their trust and their dollars into churches. Even more astounding, when Reverend Lyons resigned after the conviction, the board of the National Baptist Convention voted to continue paying him his $100,000 salary for five years, approximately the length of his sentence. It was left to a chagrined Reverend Lyons to object and say it was too much.

The culture of accepting corruption and excusing wrongdoing by black leaders as "the way we survive" has undermined the message of black ability and self-reliance. One distressingly sad example of this defeating dynamic of profiting from the problems of black people took place in a Los Angeles hospital created after the 1965 riots in the Watts neighborhood to handle the health needs in low-income black neighborhoods. It was named for two African American heroes, Dr. King and the medical pioneer Dr. Charles Drew, and the community and the hospital took pride in the fact that the majority of its staff has always been black. But forty years later a prize-winning 2004 investigation by the *Los Angeles Times* found that the hospital had long ago lost its commitment to serve people in need. Instead, the hospital became a way for people with political connections in the black community to get high-paying jobs.

Through the years, whenever the hospital's poor record of performing medical service for minorities was criticized, the response was to make shrill charges of racism and raise the memory of civil rights martyrs whose pictures hang in the lobby. Congresswoman Maxine Waters once threatened that she was willing to jump "on top of [the] desk" of one local health department official to stop any change in the way the hospital did business. She clearly was not speaking out for black people who went to the hospital for medical treatment. It was just more of the "it's the way we survive" mentality. In fact, when a proposal was made to send trauma patients to other hospitals, to give King/Drew a chance to figure out how to improve its services, Congresswoman Waters got Jesse Jackson to lead a demonstration. Jackson flew to L.A. not only to demonstrate, but also to make TV appearances to speak against any changes at a hospital that was failing poor black people. The Jackson-led rally got lots of coverage on television and featured lots of racial name-calling.

In his TV appearances, Jackson made no mention of the inferior and even deadly medical work being done on poor black and Hispanic people by the hospital. A review of the hospital's records found that it spent "inordinate sums on people who do little or no work," including spending more to pay for overtime, employee injury claims, and salaries than did nearby hospitals with double or triple the staff. Under pressure from activists who charged racism, the hospital was so richly funded by the state that it spent more per patient than any of the county's general hospitals. As for the people the hospital was supposed to serve, the paper found a record "replete with botched surgeries, misdiagnoses, and fatal neglect by nurses." The *Times* concluded, "The number of patients harmed or killed at King/Drew is impossible to tally."

In assessing the mismanagement, waste, and corruption at the hospital, a management consultant wrote that he found a dysfunctional culture in which the staff felt that they had "little incentive to do more than the 'absolute minimum to get by.'" But when local officials, black, white, and Latino, tried to reform the hospital, they encountered charges of racism. The head of the county health department was called the Grand Wizard, the title of the leader of the Ku Klux Klan. Black hospital administrators who tried to make changes to improve standards were called pawns of the white establishment and "old hog-maw-and-sauce-eatin' Negroes."

When the county supervisors held a meeting to discuss plans for reforming the hospital, Congresswoman Waters charged that racism was at work. One person in the meeting said she "hijacked the board's session by grabbing the microphone and staging a one-woman tour de force." A local civil rights lawyer said even to ask about problems at the hospital led to a "vicious, racially accusatory backlash." A county supervisor said black politicians "using the race card to prop up inferior medical standards and inferior management . . . are doing a disservice to the community." Fear of being called racist has prevented any improvement in the hospital that was created to help a community in need of medical services.

The idea of advancing the race fell off the wagon in Newark, Washington, D.C., and L.A. as self-serving political leaders retained power by keeping as their base a large population of poor and badly educated people in need and dependent. In that culture it was smart for everyone to make a personal grab for money, to hold on to power and tap into another poverty program. There was no focus on developing quality institutions and leaders for black America. And Jesse Jackson and Al Sharpton took the same political model to the national level with their ability to get TV time and pressure corporations as the base of their claim to be national black leaders. They used the TV time to add to their fame, and the access to corporate leaders to make deals for themselves and their friends. Lost in the mix was the idea of leading people to educate themselves, to strengthen their job opportunities, and focus on the value of a solid family. The fundamental premise of black political leadership shared by the roll call of great black leaders in the past—Booker T. Washington and Frederick Douglass, W.E.B. DuBois and Dr. King, Thurgood Marshall and grassroots leaders like Fannie Lou Hamer and Malcolm X—was abandoned in favor of something weaker, less morally certain, and often counterproductive. Too many of today's black leaders have less to do with "blood of martyrs" than with "blood money," the equivalent of the thirty pieces of silver handed to Judas, the biblical traitor.

3

THE REPARATIONS MIRAGE

BEFORE BILL COSBY DARED to speak out, the most controversial idea in black America was a demand for financial reparations for slavery. Even after Cosby called for black people to account for not taking full advantage of fifty years of new opportunities opened by the *Brown* decision, serious people spent time discussing reparations, a divisive, dead-end idea.

Reparations head the agenda of today's left-wing black activists. They were demanded by the leaders of both Million Man March demonstrations. Rastafarians holding their annual meeting in 2005 put them at the top of their agenda. College debates on reparations continue to draw big crowds. Congressman John Conyers, a Michigan Democrat, continues a quixotic push, started in 1989, to get the U.S. government to study the economic impact of slavery as a first step toward reparation payments. And the combination of satisfying racial justice and a big-money payday has attracted high-powered lawyers including Harvard Law School professor Charles Ogletree, and successful private counsel such as Willie Gary and the late Johnnie Cochran.

Mainstream black organizations, such as the NAACP, have

fallen under the spell of the reparations movement. Speaking at the 2005 NAACP convention, Dennis Hayes, the chief executive officer of the NAACP, said his group was joining with reparations advocates to demand money from companies with any history of involvement in slavery. "Many of the problems we have now, including poverty, disparities in health care, and incarcerations can be directly tied to slavery," he said.

Hayes did not explain his argument—or explain how reparations would fix these problems. He didn't have to. Hayes and many other hip black leaders take it for granted that black people deserve reparations. Without a thought, they have made it a staple of today's black politics that black people remain defined as victims, who should be paid reparations now, when most black Americans do not live in poverty, are not in jail, and reign as the wealthiest black people in the world.

This is the heart of the "blacks as victims" mentality, the logic that defines black people as completely powerless, ill-educated, and emotionally damaged. So, by this reasoning, how can someone like Bill Cosby ask poor black people to account for their actions as parents, as educators, as politicians, as rappers, and as civil rights leaders if they are all victims? When Cosby publicly calls for black Americans, especially the black poor, to take control of the amazing opportunities within their reach fifty years after *Brown*, he is crossing an invisible line in permissible public speech, breaking the taboo against ever telling white people that slavery is history. Slavery was a scandalous crime that nevertheless proved that strong black people can rise above any hurdle, in the hard-earned tradition of self-reliance. Instead, the agreed message among self-described progressive black leaders is that white people are in control of all the problems facing black America. And it follows, by this twisted logic, that white people owe a debt to black people because of slavery, and white people are never to be allowed to get out of that burden. That is why Cosby was accused of revealing secrets, hanging dirty laundry out in public, and failing to understand the impact of structural racism.

A poisonous message for black people hides in that line of thinking, one that is particularly damaging to the black poor, struggling for education and opportunity: Whites have all the power, you are weak, you can't make a difference for yourself or your family, and you will always be a victim. There is an unfortunate message for the rest of America, too: Assumptions about black American inferiority are true, since immigrants from Asia and the Balkans are not asking for anything. They are glad to get into the United States to be free to seek economic opportunities. Africans fleeing war and political oppression are not asking for anything from the government. They ask only for a chance to get to America, and then compete and make it in America.

Cosby's genius was in striking at the heart of this corrupt network of assumptions. These are the quiet, unspoken assumptions, the private thoughts and whispers that feed racism, anger, and distrust on all sides, slowing the steady progress black people have made over centuries in America. Ironically, for all the damage it leaves in its wake, the reparations movement is making scant progress in the worlds of politics or the courts, much less in the halls of Congress. The movement is going nowhere. It is a self-indulgent waste of time. So, why is the call for reparations still the battle cry of so many black leaders? That compelling question extends beyond Bill Cosby's challenge to black people to break free from the self-imposed chains of mental slavery, the acceptance of being a victim. The failure to liberate black minds rests on a tragic misreading of the source of strength that is the basis of pride in blackness and the greatness of black American history.

Black people fought to be equals even when slavery was legal. They risked their lives to lead revolts, to escape and build secret networks for others to escape. Black men demanded to be put in uniform to fight against the Confederacy that wanted to continue slavery. And black people built their own schools, churches, and businesses once they were free. They insisted on being seen as equal citizens of the nation, free from stereotypes of weakness that white people would try to put on them, slanders about ignorance, laziness, and incompetence in the most basic human skill: to love and raise a family. Able, smart, and defiant black leaders battled for years against segregation and won the *Brown* decision that opened more opportunities for a free, confident, self-reliant people. The power and will of black people from Sojourner Truth to Frederick Douglass defies the idea that people who lived under slavery were necessarily crippled. The lesson of slavery for black people is, ironically, about how perseverance and strength and unbendable dedication to a goal can lead, ultimately, to victory.

Reparations, on the other hand, require black Americans to embrace a self-image of weakness and take on the cloak of a broken people. It asks contemporary black Americans to cash in on the exploitation of long-dead slaves by long-dead slave masters. Yes, it is a fact that black people had their labor stolen from them by slavery. America's black slaves never got paid for 246 years of backbreaking work. Their craftsmanship and raw physical labor, used for everything from picking cotton to building the U.S. Capitol, were never compensated with a paycheck.

But those ancestors are dead. They are not here to pick up their wages. They have left us a valuable inheritance, however. The world can see their legacy as a strong, creative, loving people who survived the Middle Passage, the whip, and rank oppression to leave an inspiring history. The music, religion, food, dance, sport, and defiant spirit of the African American slaves can be found in the fiber of American history and identity. Their story is at the heart of America's struggle to live up to the ideals of liberty and justice for all.

Let's review the history that leads to the call for reparations. There is no question about the horror of slavery. It was a bloody, criminal enterprise and a mark of shame on the new nation, America's original sin. Hypocritical founding fathers spoke of liberty, but made slavery legal. In fact, eight of the nation's first twelve presidents owned slaves. President Thomas Jefferson, who conceived of the Bill of Rights, owned slaves. That apparently included his lover, Sally Hemmings. But there was no family inheritance for children of mixed parentage. And there was no paycheck for labor, for skilled work with animals and tools, or for the mastery of farming required of slaves to make a successful business of a plantation. Black slaves were not paid for their work.

The truth is that giving reparations to slaves was first a white man's idea. President Lincoln wanted to create a fund to help slaves who lacked education, jobs, and homes get started on life as free people. The money was to be given to state governments based on their slave population. Lincoln's assassination killed that idea as well. The federal government never acted on it. Another offer of reparations came from General William Sherman of the Union Army. He offered forty-acre parcels of land to former slaves. At the end of the Civil War, the slave population was free but obviously destitute, lacking schools, jobs, and a place to live. General Sherman's plan was to give the newly emancipated slaves land that had belonged to Confederate plantation owners along the Georgia and Carolina coastlines. The general later added to the deal by offering the use of army mules to former slaves who needed draft animals to help plow the land. More than forty thousand former slaves moved onto the land in the six months after the initial offer in January 1865. But President Andrew Johnson, trying to keep the country together in the aftermath of the Civil War, decided to return the land to the white former slave masters and had the former slaves evicted. This is the legendary "forty acres and a mule," the broken promise to former slaves that is at the base of today's reparations movement. The rap group Public Enemy asked in one early-nineties song: "Forty Acres and a mule, Jack / Where is it at? Why'd you try to fool the Black?" *Essence* magazine had an economist estimate the value of "forty acres and a mule" in 1993 dollars, and it came to $43,209.

So, in addition to the centuries-long horrors of slavery, newly emancipated slaves were immediately bamboozled out of promised reparations. Still, the push for reparations for slavery today requires a leap in logic. Since there are no living former slaves, the advocates of reparations have to make black Americans today into victims of slavery. Otherwise the statute of limitations has long since expired on any claim for reparations. This requires that black people agree to act the part of an inferior, weak people who are still flat on their backs, permanently defeated by the damage done by slavery several generations ago.

Reparations advocates, notably Randall Robinson, author of the best-selling book *The Debt: What America Owes to Blacks*, argue that current high levels of poverty, bad schools, poor credit, high unemployment, even the troubling rate of infant mortality among black children, are the direct results of slavery. Robinson's stretch across thin ice requires him to merge slavery with all the history that followed it. He starts with feet firmly rooted in history that has freed slaves becoming sharecroppers, working for little money, if any, because they had few options. Robinson is right when he says former slaves were denied equal rights through acts of intimidation against them, including lynching, which often went unpunished by local or federal law enforcement. He rightly notes that federal laws—in violation of the Constitution—made it legal to treat black people as second-class citizens, subject to discrimination in education and hiring, often denied the right to vote. Black businesses faced rampant discrimination, which meant that equity in homes and businesses, a key building block to wealth, was denied black Americans.

Where Robinson skates off the edge of an interesting argument and into a dangerous, self-abasing fantasy is in attaching the impact of slavery to the years beyond 1954 and the *Brown* decision. In the half-century since *Brown*, the levels of black education, income, and political power have all grown, evidence that most black people are taking advantage of newly opened doors. Today, half of all black families are middle-class, earning at least twice as much as the poverty line. Only one percent of African American families made that claim in 1940. Rates of college graduation have skyrocketed. To make the argument that slavery is responsible for today's social and economic problems facing poor black people is to take away all of their personal will, diminish their independence, and dismiss their intellect. And how can he explain the fact that at the start of the twentieth century black people had higher marriage rates than whites? In 1940 the out-of-wedlock birth rate for blacks was 19 percent. Today it is close to 70 percent. If slavery is the cause of today's social problems in the black community, why did black people in closer historical proximity to it do better than today's black community with regard to keeping families together?

And the reparations movement also requires that America's whites, Latinos, and immigrants from around the world buy into the idea of a collective national guilt over slavery. Today even most white Americans can accurately say their ancestors had nothing to do with slavery.

To prop up their weak argument, reparations advocates are quick to point out that the U.S. government has paid reparations to Japanese Americans and a small number of black people, too. The U.S. Congress voted in 1988 to pay $20,000 per person to each of the 60,000 Japanese Americans still living who were interned during World War II. That payment is along the lines of the $58 billion that the German government has paid in reparations to more than 500,000 Jewish survivors of the Holocaust. Closer to the idea of reparations for slavery, the Florida legislature has paid $150,000 to eight black people, the only living survivors of white racist attacks in 1923 that left twenty-six black people dead in the small black community of Rosewood. The legislature also provided $500,000 to compensate African American families who lost property during the attacks on black homes, churches, and businesses.

Similarly, an Oklahoma commission has backed reparations for victims of a 1921 attack by white racists that devastated the black business section of Tulsa and killed three hundred people. But no reparations were paid. The state legislature limited action to a simple formal apology.

The problem with all the examples is that reparations money went to living victims of the crimes—be it the Holocaust, internment, or racial violence. The current reparations movement has to deal with the absence of living victims of slavery. That is why Randall Robinson feels the need to blame all the problems facing black people today on slavery. In addition, several courts have ruled that the statute of limitations has expired on claims by the few remaining children or grandchildren of slaves. That is why reparations supporters are trying to make every black man and woman into a victim.

The best argument for reparations was outlined by a group of prominent and affluent black lawyers that included the late Johnnie Cochran. They made the case that the U.S. government failed to protect the rights and property of black people after slavery. It is called the "due process" argument, because the Fourteenth Amendment to the Constitution, written after the Civil War, guarantees all Americans equal protection under law and the right to due process in court regardless of their race. The U.S. government broke the law by failing to protect the personal rights and the property of freed slaves. Congress and the courts allowed state and local governments to discriminate against black people, and the Supreme Court ruled that the denial of equal rights was legal. As attorney Richard F. Scruggs said in a *Harper's* magazine roundtable on reparations in 2001: "You know what's nice about [the idea of a] due-process lawsuit. It does away with a lot of complaints that 'We Were Also Done Wrong,' from the Irish or other minorities, precisely because it recognizes the fundamental difference. African Americans were kept down by the force of law, not custom, and then every effort to lift the burden of the law was met with denial of due process."

But even the due-process argument has a hard row to hoe. First, slavery was legal in the United States until the Emancipation Proclamation. How is it possible to sue a businessman over a lawful act of business? Second, even if it was a crime against humanity, the statute of limitations for prosecuting slaveholders—the actual criminals—has long expired. And the slaveholders are dead. Their money has been dispersed across generations. There can be no exact accounting of what happened to the money that came from their thievery. As a result, some supporters of reparations have turned to lawsuits far away from slaveholders. One man sued the Democratic Party. Reverend Wayne Perryman of Seattle's Mount Calvary Christian Center Church of God in Christ has filed two lawsuits against Democrats. He said the political party dominated the South during slavery and made it a key part of their platform, so they should pay reparations. Another possible target for this slippery argument is all of American business. A bank that financed a plantation might be liable. A newspaper that ran an ad offering slaves for sale or an insurance company that insured slaves as property is open to be sued under this attenuated theory. Other targets include railroads that transported goods produced by slaves, and manufacturing companies that turned slave-picked cotton into shirts, blankets, and other textiles. A few city councils in urban areas with large black populations, such as Detroit, Philadelphia, and Chicago, have passed laws that require all businesses to file reports on their past relationship to slavery before they can get city contracts. The state of California also has a slavery disclosure law. That has led some companies to issue convoluted apologies. J.P. Morgan Chase Bank, after a study of its corporate roots, found that it long ago bought out two banks in Louisiana that had financed mortgages on plantations in the early 1800s, and when those loans defaulted, the company ended up with slaves as collateral. Morgan Chase apologized and announced a scholarship program for students in Louisiana.

Lawsuits against the companies, however, went nowhere. In July 2005 a federal judge said slavery caused "tremendous suffering and ineliminable scars" but said any attempt to get money from corporations, such as J.P. Morgan, "more than a century after the end of the Civil War and the formal abolition of slavery fails." The judge, Charles R. Norgle, said the burden was on the people bringing the suit to prove they suffered personal injuries from slavery, and that a genealogical tie to a slave did not rise to the level of personal injury. He raised another devilish point for the reparations advocates. What suffering did black people with slaves in their family's past encounter that was not also felt by black people without any ties to slaves? And the judge noted, as others had done before, that the statute of limitations had long run out on slavery claims. So the lawsuit was too late and based on too little. Norgle's ruling came ten years after the most liberal federal court in the nation, California's Ninth Circuit, threw out a reparations lawsuit seeking $100 million, also on the grounds that too much time had passed and there were no legal grounds for suing the U.S. government over slavery.

The judges in theses cases didn't mention it, but there are some outstanding questions, even if they had given the go-ahead to reparations. The most important question is how will poor black people—whose plight is cited as the basis for the suit—be helped by reparations money? Will it remove stubborn pockets of poverty in which black people are manacled by low-quality schools, high rates of such social ills as AIDS and drug addiction, and too many broken families? Maybe that doesn't matter to reparations advocates dead set on making someone pay. For some the reparations argument is a legitimate argument about setting the historical record straight, finding a way toward truth and reconciliation about this country's bloody racial history. But for some others, pushing the reparations issue seems to be about exploiting the blood and sweat of slaves and the problems of impoverished black people for the purpose of putting money in their own pockets. In other words, some are conjuring the suffering of our ancestors as a way to scam poor people today.

In November 2004 a federal jury in Oxford, Mississippi, convicted Morris James on twenty-three counts of fraud for taking $431,000 from more than six thousand low-income black people by charging them to prepare fraudulent tax returns claiming reparations for slavery. When James was charged in 2003, the Justice Department also obtained court orders to stop five other people from selling schemes to get reparations as part of tax returns. In 2000 and 2001, the Internal Revenue Service said it paid out more than $30 million by mistake to people who falsely claimed to be eligible for slavery reparations tax credits. That follows in the path of Robert Brock, who for years barnstormed through the South making speeches at small black churches offering to file tax forms claiming $500,000 in reparations payments for individual black people if they first paid him a fifty-dollar fee. He made reparations for slavery the answer to every conspiracy theory launched against black people. He particularly blamed Jews and Hispanics and Arabs for the problems of black people, and announced that he was in agreement with white separatists who wanted blacks to go back to Africa. As crazy as all that seems, Brock got 165,000 people to hand over fifty dollars before the government caught up with him.

When the judges on the Ninth Circuit dismissed the 1995 reparations lawsuit, they said slavery was an atrocity and pointed to Congress, a political institution, not the courts, as the right body to look at any call for reparations. But in Congress, as in the increasingly diverse population of the United States, there is no momentum to offer compensation to black Americans for slavery. In fact there is a steady, resolute opposition to any effort even to study the issue. In every Congress since 1989, Representative John Conyers, a black Michigan Democrat, has reintroduced a bill calling for a federal study of reparations. In the years since then, there have been three presidents—one Democrat and two Republicans—and control of the Congress has shifted from

Democrats to Republicans. But neither party has acted on the bill in the Congress, and presidents George H. W. Bush, Bill Clinton, and George W. Bush have not shown a shred of interest in it. More than simple indifference is at work here. Illinois Republican Henry Hyde, the former chairman of the House Judiciary Committee, apparently spoke for his colleagues when he was asked about the possibility of Congress approving reparations for slavery. "The notion of collective guilt for what people did [more than two hundred] years ago, that this generation should pay a debt for that generation, is an idea whose time has gone. I never owned a slave. I never oppressed anybody." Some critics of reparations go even further. Writing in *American Enterprise* magazine, Karl Zinsmeister argued that any debt over slavery had been paid with the blood of the people who died in the Civil War to end slavery. "In all, more than 620,000 Americans died in the struggle to eliminate slavery. That is more than the number killed in all of our other wars combined. . . . The crux that defined and drove this ferocious fratricide was determination to purge ourselves of slavery. . . . Our nation surely did run up a debt for allowing black bondage. But that bill was finally paid off in blood." And then there is the black writer John McWhorter, who points out that that black African kings sold most slaves (prisoners captured in tribal wars) to the whites who shipped them to the Americas. Should African nations pay reparations? It is also true that most whites alive during the time of slavery never owned slaves. And there were thousands of blacks in America who owned slaves. That leads to another awful question: Should the descendants of black slave owners be eligible for reparations? Should the families of whites who never owned slaves be charged? What about families with mixed racial heritage?

Those attitudes and questions—some more credible than

others—are a good representation of the nation's unease with the idea of reparations. In 2001, nearly 70 percent of white Americans told a Gallup poll that they opposed even an official government apology for slavery. In 2005 the U.S. Senate could not get a unanimous vote on an apology for years of failing to pass anti-lynching legislation. A 2002 Gallup poll found that 90 percent of white Americans opposed reparations, as did half of black Americans. To repeat, half of all black Americans are opposed to the idea of accepting a free check for reparations. Obviously there is no political base for building a strong movement for reparations in the United States. Some cities with sizable black populations will ask for big companies to do studies of the issue, but even those cities will not pay to do the studies themselves, much less agree to pay reparations for slavery out of their own treasuries.

The fact that so many black people don't want reparations is a challenge to even the highest aims of people backing reparations—people who want to put reparations checks into a national fund for black people. Randall Robinson and Tulane law professor Robert Westley, among others, have embraced the altruistic idea of using money from reparations to create a national trust to start black businesses and improve schools for black children. Henry Louis Gates Jr., the former head of the Afro-American studies department at Harvard University, has an even larger vision. He wants countries that engaged in the slave trade to forgive the debts of African nations. These ideas represent opportunities for black elites to take control of poverty programs aimed at poor black people and foreign policy plans for black nations. In both cases, selected black people will replace policymakers and government administrators at the controls of billions of dollars. Picking the lucky black people who get to be paid to run these programs is an unanswered problem. So, too, is the question of who sets the policy. Is this the start of a separate black nation with a separate black elected leadership and a separate black foreign policy? Scandals are sure to follow as money goes to people who are friends of the people handing out the money. And it is to be expected that dissident camps of black nationalists will complain that whoever is controlling the money is addressing the wrong need.

The good of these ideas is that they move reparations away from the stigma of a get-rich-quick scheme for some black people. There is a telling flaw, however. Robinson has conceded that a reparations fund will not help the black poor. The beneficiaries will be the black middle class. In one startlingly honest interview, he said the black middle class needs the money because "so many of us, a disproportionate many, are first-generation college graduates. We have no financial assets." In other words, the money represents capital for investments, for buying houses, land, and starting black-owned businesses. That version of reparations is sure to unleash unprecedented levels of capital for black entrepreneurs. Imagine Bob Johnson, the founder of Black Entertainment Television, pooling investment capital from his associates' reparations checks. Imagine the growth in the stock portfolios of the black upper class. One major reparations supporter, Chicago alderman Carrie Austin, has made it clear that the reparations question in the twenty-first century is no longer about slavery or even the idea that the problems of today's poor black Americans are tied to slavery. It is about wealth. "I want forty acres and a Lexus," she famously said. "You can keep the mule."

On that level, reparations are about a politically powerful black middle class demanding to be paid for the sins of America's past. African Americans today, with a record number of elected officials in Congress and in local government (such as Alderman Carrie Austin), are in position to make demands on American government and corporations. They have the power to attract attention for those titillating demands in newspapers and on television as well as in academia. This is chest-thumping by the best-educated and most politically powerful group of black people in history. As Randall Robinson told the *Washington Post* after his book was published, it does not matter if Congress and corporations never write the first check for reparations. What matters is that black people "have decided for ourselves that (reparations) are our due." That is fine as a matter of political drama and even as a strategy for gaining leverage for larger political fights. But all that is easily lost on troubled souls who hear in the rhetoric of their leaders that the cry for reparations is a call for justice because they remain victimized due to slavery. At bottom, reparations today are advertised as an update on the 1865 concept of giving newly freed slaves a start in life after emancipation, with the modern recipients being all black people in the name of the poorest, most damaged black people. In this frame of thinking, the most dysfunctional, badly educated, even criminal black person is hailed as truly black and the inspiration for reparations. This is a perversion of the truth. At its very best, the reparations argument is a political strategy with a deadly cost attached for people who can't see what is going on and that they—poor, young black people—are being sacrificed for a one-time payout.

The reparations movement today is a lot like the government's offer of reservations to Native Americans. Just as the government pushed Native Americans into isolation and out of the mainstream of American life, reparations are an invitation to increase racial segregation and isolation of low-income black people. A one-time payment is sure to be an easy out for the government. It is cheaper than annual funding for social programs to deal with the ongoing horrors of bad schools, jails overflowing with young black people, and a rising number of children born into poverty because they are born to unmarried young mothers.

For black people the real cost for reparations is not a matter of money. The real price is removing all moral responsibility from white Americans for the nation's historic ill treatment of black people. White guilt is the trigger of the ongoing national consensus that America has to invest in repairing the damage done by racism. Once the check is written, once the "debt" is paid, there will be an end to white guilt and to America's obligation to invest in helping poor black people find their strength and stand on their own feet. The idea of civic engagement to promote good race relations will be gone. It is telling that two very conservative white columnists have embraced the idea of the U.S. government issuing reparations checks to all black people. Charles Krauthammer and Zev Chafets have concluded in separate writings that they support reparations if it means an end to affirmative action programs for colleges, jobs, and contracts. They are glad to offer reparations if they cancel future spending on social programs to eradicate racial inequities in housing, health care, and more. America's power structure will be off the hook for all time in regard to opening the doors of the old boys' club. If government, academia, and private industry are given a free pass, the segregation of poor black people will escalate rapidly. The segregation of the poorest black people will increase and be set in stone, to the point of permanent isolation. This is not a good deal. It is a trap. Some may say it is a gold-plated trap. It is still a trap.

Martin Luther King Jr. famously appealed to white Americans to open the doors to opportunity and extend a hand to help the disadvantaged enter into the mainstream. This is black America's family jewel—the moral leverage that comes from a proud people engaging in a just struggle for human rights after suffering the horror of slavery and legal discrimination. To sell that treasure for a reparations check is to sell out, and cheaply. Black people have a legitimate claim on the nation's conscience and resources as fellow citizens. Why start begging? Think about what we as black people are saying to our own children: that we believe we are weaker than any Bosnian refugee recently uprooted by genocide. Are we weaker than any one of the "Lost Boys of Sudan," thousands of miles from home and culture, but working to adjust in a land free of tyranny? Are we really willing to say that any black American is weaker in mind and spirit than any Mexican who left a small village for the chance to hustle two jobs in Chicago and send some money home? Those people are victims of abuse. They have lived through oppression and political upheaval. And yet they are not asking for anything but a chance to get an education and a job and compete in the world's greatest economy, America.

Reparations send a message to Americans of every other race that blacks are wards of the state because they are a broken people. Social ills in the black community would be exaggerated as black people, flush with one big check, decide they don't need school, don't need a job, and remove themselves from the vitality of mainstream American life. Black people would be more highly stigmatized and stereotyped than ever before.

The suffering of ancestors is not a claim ticket for a bag full of cash. Who wants money in their pocket that is stained with the blood of slaves? That is obscene. The great civil rights struggle has always been for the right to an equal opportunity to compete. Being equal requires the confidence that comes from knowing you have earned your way, even against great odds and injustice.

Even if most black Americans today could prove that their ancestors were American slaves, and that is doubtful, the labor of ancestors three, four, and five generations gone cannot prove the worth of black people living in the twenty-first century. Each generation, each man and each woman, has to make its own mark on history, punch its own ticket.

Black leadership needs to invest its energy in programs to bring big-city schools out of crisis. The black nation has to get busy forming coalitions with Hispanics, immigrants, and other big-city minorities to get local, state, and national governments to work for them.

Instead, there are marches, meetings, and books about reparations. The reparations movement is a flashy distraction from the real work black America needs to do to take advantage of a nation that has more opportunities for black people than ever. All reparations can do is diminish white guilt as well as black pride. There is no dollar value attached to the debt the nation owes to slaves buried long ago. The inheritance is pride that comes from knowing our black ancestors persevered through hell to fight for their rights in this country. Black history is not about selling out for a quick check that is a lure to increased segregation, self-pity, and lowered standards for competing in a global economy. Black history is all about daring, strong men and women competing in the mainstream of American life and winning. Bill Cosby is in line with the greats of black history when he calls for black people, even those with the heaviest struggles, to tap into the power of black pride in success. The reparations movement is a detour into self-abasing pity. And it is bad strategy. There are no shortcuts on the road to justice and equality for all.

4

THE RADICAL GOAL OF EDUCATION

WHAT THE HELL GOOD is *Brown v. Board of Education* if nobody wants it?"

That question stands as the central challenge from Bill Cosby's controversial speech on the fiftieth anniversary of the *Brown* decision. Admittedly, on its face the question is ridiculous.

No credible leader in American public life, black or white, right-wing or left-wing, is taking a stand against the *Brown* decision. Conservative Supreme Court nominees speak against activist liberal courts and bite their tongues about *Roe v. Wade* (the decision that legalized abortion). But they pay tribute to high-court activism when it comes to the *Brown* decision. Today even the white Southern segregationists who fought to stop it have long since ceased trying to make the case that black children have no right to well-funded public schools. It is as American as "one man, one vote" to say that every child deserves a chance for a good education. Like it or not, *Brown* is publicly honored as a knockout punch, the case that settled the argument over legal school segregation. White Americans may not be hugely enthusiastic about integrated schools; poll numbers continue to show that most white people do not want to send their children to schools with a large percentage of black children. But there is no call from white America for the Supreme Court to reverse *Brown* and return to officially segregated schools.

Black Americans, on the other hand, have every reason to celebrate *Brown*. It stands as the mountaintop triumph, the moment in American history when centuries of struggle were rewarded and the walls of legal American segregation began to crumble. Allowing black children access to better schools is the foundation of today's black middle class, the most affluent and politically powerful black population in world history.

Before, during, and after slavery, black Americans looked to education as their salvation. It was the way out, a star of hope that offered them an equal chance to succeed. In the antebellum era, Southern slave owners denied blacks the right to learn how to read as a tactic to enforce black inferiority. Lack of literacy protected slave owners against any informed, thoughtful black mind that might speak of freedom, organize rebellions, or, most daring of all, compete with white people.

After the Civil War, black people put what few resources they had into the creation of schools. The federal government also focused on educating the freed slaves. That led to fierce opposition from white segregationists. In addition to all of the other reasons that held sway during slavery, they opposed education because educated black people created a political threat to white political power. Educating blacks would undermine tactics—such as "literacy tests"—that white southerners used to deny black people the right to vote. This opposition only added a sense of urgency to black efforts to gain an education. "The opposition to Negro education in the South was at first bitter, and showed itself in ashes, insult, and blood," wrote W.E.B. DuBois in *The Souls of*

Black Folk. "For the South believed an educated Negro to be a dangerous Negro. And the South was not wholly wrong; for education among all kinds of men always has had and always will have an element of danger and revolution, of dissatisfaction and discontent. Nevertheless, men strive to know."

To appreciate what education meant to freed slaves, it is important to know that in a thirty-year period, between 1880 and 1910, the percentage of black people who could read and write jumped from 30 percent to 70 percent. This rapid rise in black literacy took place despite a lack of schools, frequent denial of the right to vote, and intimidation of any black person who dared to run for office, including seats on the school boards that controlled funding for black schools. Ku Klux Klan activity during the same period included targeted attacks on black schoolhouses. As a result, teaching took place in churches, under the guise of learning the word of God from the Bible, but also in social clubs, and after work. Black people took a risk to get an education. Education was a radical tool of liberation for black people so recently enslaved and purposely denied the chance to learn. To be able to read and write was a sign of self-determination, of strength. A man or woman who could read was a cut above, clearly focused on leaving cultural and educational capital for their children, even if they had no monetary wealth to pass on. "Educate! Educate! Educate! Get all the knowledge within reach and then use it for the good of the race," J. Max Barber, a black journalist, wrote in 1905.

In the first part of the twentieth century, before *Brown* exposed the lie of "separate but equal," the few schools for black children featured overcrowded classrooms. The teachers generally had little more than a bare-bones education to offer their students. Those black teachers did have a reputation for being loving and committed to their work, seeing it as a critical part of the race's larger crusade for justice. But they were paid less than white teachers and given little to work with. School buildings for black children looked like shacks compared with the facilities for white students. In black schools, students had no books at all or left-over, out-of-date textbooks collected after being discarded by the white schools. Black students usually did not go beyond the eighth grade because that was where their schools stopped. The accepted logic was that no servant, farmhand, or messenger needed more education than that. Few black children had the lux-ury of even going to these poor-cousin schools because their fam-ilies needed them to work from an early age. If they did go to school, the black children most often walked while the white chil-dren rode buses to school. This reality was the cornerstone of segregationist efforts to limit and control black Americans and keep alive a tradition of racial oppression rooted in slavery.

Which is why it is such a shock, a century later, to find Bill Cosby talking to black people, not whites, when he puts the chal-lenge on the table: "What the hell good is *Brown* if nobody wants it?"

There is no doubt that he is talking about black children who don't go to school or drop out of school; he is talking about a cul-ture that openly demeans any black student who achieves aca-demic excellence as inauthentic and acting white; he is talking about a culture that accepts going to jail as normal; he is talking about black parents who accept excuses instead of demanding top grades from their children.

"Well, *Brown v. Board of Education*, where are we today?" Cosby asked in pained frustration during his Constitution Hall speech. "It's there. They [civil rights leaders of fifty years ago] paved the way. What did we do with it? The white man, he's laughing, got to be laughing. Fifty percent dropout rate, rest of them in prison."

Cosby is talking specifically about the disregard for educa-tion that is too often part of the social outlook of poorer black

Americans—often because of the failure of their leaders to make the historical struggle for education relevant in their lives. Cosby spoke direct words of warning while official black leaders remain silent as part of a strategy that allows them to claim they shared being victims of racism with the black poor, even though the leadership is distinctly middle class and well educated, and frequently sends its children to elite private schools.

That leaves poor black people open to a massive lie—that education is no big deal. After all, poor black children are most vulnerable to the poisonous idea that that excellence in school is for whites or black nerds. That idea is one of the main ingredients of America's minstrel-show popular culture. Black characters on TV and in music videos dazzle with ripped muscles, blunt profanity, and brandished guns, but not mental power. The vast majority of "powerful" black people to whom black children are exposed in our popular culture are rapping, telling dirty jokes, acting like gangbangers, playing basketball or football, or are menacing criminals in jail. There is a seductive, serpentine logic at work on young black people. Without anyone saying a word, black youngsters find themselves in a hypnotic, self-defeating trance that has them walking blindly into a back alley of failure. Brainwashed by popular culture to ignore reality, they are in a confused state of mind and doubt the value of schooling. When they watch TV or listen to music they never see people who have succeeded on the basis of education—black intellectuals, artists, and professionals such as dentists, lawyers, and doctors—celebrated for their accomplishments. In fact, people with that kind of success are ignored, if not put down as not authentically black, because they don't fit the caricature of black people in the culture.

In a speech after his controversial remarks at the *Brown* gala, Cosby mentioned the important role of educated black people in winning the *Brown* case. He noted that black athletes had, at that point in history, jumped "longer, farther, higher," and been champion boxers as well as outstanding tennis, basketball, and baseball players. But when it was time to argue for school integration, he said, "we didn't take people who could jump higher, run faster . . . we took our historically black college educated lawyers and went up against the racists . . . I'm talking to you about how we did it with our brains."

Cosby remains convinced that black intellectual ability is not celebrated by black people, and especially by black parents, as they raise children. In an interview for this book, he told the story of how a school system gave extra money every month to the parents of children with learning disabilities. An Alabama mother got an extra $500 to help with her child, who remained mute for his first several years in school. One day a teacher saw the child talking loudly in a supermarket. The mother spied the shocked teacher and ran to the child. She began smacking him and telling him that if he kept speaking in public, she couldn't get her monthly check. "She is teaching that child there is no value in education, but there is money to be made in ignorance," said Cosby. This story may sound like an urban legend, similar to Ronald Reagan's "welfare queen" stories in the 1980s, but it's noteworthy that it sounds credible to black ears.

Rejecting the value of school has numerous consequences: children end up not learning standard English, not writing well, and, worst of all, accepting the idea of failure. "*Brown v. Board of Education* is no longer the white person's problem," said Cosby, making it clear he was talking to black America's leadership about the crisis created by a culture among poor black people that turns away from education. Cosby said nobody talks to teachers, but teachers tell him that the language spoken by black children coming into classrooms today is "horrible."

This horror show—a refusal to master standard English, a

lack of interest in formal schooling, the acceptance of a culture of failure—is passed on to children and grandchildren as a legacy of being authentically black, when really it is a legacy of failure. And the tide of failure keeps rising, drowning soul after soul. The tragedy is blamed on white people, racism, or even abandonment by the black middle class. Yet there is no leadership speaking out to black parents and black students about the destructive cycle rooted in a crippling culture that sells disregard for education. No one is sounding the alarm to say the house is on fire, and black people, especially poor black people, are being left behind in a global competition for jobs that demands the highest level of academic achievement.

This silence reveals one of two things. It is either the case that civil rights leaders believe that the one-third of black people who remain locked in poverty—despite all the new doors opened in the fifty years since *Brown*—are beyond hope, or civil rights leaders are afraid to challenge black people who are profiting from the system, including members of teachers' unions, big-city school boards, and the political class of superintendents and city councils. Cosby said as much when he complained about "poverty pimps," black leaders making money off the problems of poor black people: "These are the first ones to start screaming because they knew when they heard what I was saying that there was a chance they would lose their gig." And that is why he spoke out to black parents urging them to take personal responsibility for educating their children. "People in the neighborhood have to teach people where they are [inflicting damage on themselves and their children] and you do this through word of mouth, through example," Cosby said.

There is no disputing the facts of educational failure in black America fifty years after *Brown*. Only 50 percent of black students who enter the ninth grade later graduate with a regular high school diploma. The sad but real 50-percent graduation rate is far below the 75 percent of white students who get a regular diploma, according to a 2004 study by the Civil Rights Project at Harvard University and the Urban Institute. They found that the black high school graduation rate was even lower than the 53-percent rate of Hispanic students, many of them recent immigrants who face a language barrier as they go to U.S. schools. But what is more troubling is that hidden within the 50 percent graduation rate for black students is an even lower graduation rate for black males. Only 43 percent of black boys graduate from high school with a regular diploma.

This scandal of modern education is hidden in official graduation rates that claim black students aged eighteen to twenty-four have a high school completion rate of 84 percent. That is lower than the 92-percent completion rate for whites, but it is not alarming. Those rates, however, include GEDs (General Educational Development degrees) and attendance certificates that obscure the sad reality of how few black children, especially boys, are getting a real high school education.

By every measure there has been a big jump in high school graduation rates for black Americans since 1950. But if you ask any black person who got out of high school before 1954 about the quality of education they got in segregated high schools, they speak with pride about defying segregation with a high level of achievement in an environment of demanding black teachers. When they compare their education with what is going on in predominantly black schools in the big city today, they speak with regret.

Before the *Brown* decision, only 24 percent of blacks under age thirty had finished high school, about half the rate for white Americans. Initially, school integration opened doors to better schools for more black people. Large numbers of black Americans who had been held back by segregation jumped to get their diplomas and that has pushed up the official graduation rate.

But that progress has now been stalled for more than twenty years. Official graduation rates for blacks have not significantly changed since 1982. Something terrible has happened, and school officials have been hiding this festering rot behind flimsy claims that 84 percent of black students get some version of a high school certificate. The fact is that many of those high school degrees are worthless in a competitive global economy. According to federal data, the average black American twelfth grader scores worse on basic skills than 80 percent of white twelfth graders. That is a serious gap. It is a mortal threat to the race.

That gap is evident in grades and test scores. For example, a 1997 College Board report on high school seniors headed to college found that only 19 percent of black seniors said they have an A average. That compares to 30 percent of Hispanics who reported they were A students, 40 percent of whites, and 47.5 percent of Asians. On standardized tests, the same gap appears. In 2004 the gap between black and white students on the verbal part of the test was 98 points. On the math part of the test the gap was 104 points.

As a group, black students in the twelfth grade actually score lower on reading tests than eighth grade whites. The same is true in math, history, and geography. Overall, more than 40 percent of black high school seniors tested below the basic skill level in reading, according to the National Assessment for Educational Progress. Nearly 70 percent of the black seniors scored below the basic level in math and nearly 80 percent in science. That is a stark contrast to the 75 percent of whites scoring above the basic level in math and 63 percent of whites above level in the sciences.

There is no dispute that the train is off the tracks, the house is on fire, and the dirty laundry is pushing out of the closet. Yet no black leader is willing to say there is a yawning gap between blacks and whites in terms of the intellectual skills and knowledge their children are taking away from high school. This silence, this refusal to say the emperor has no clothes, keeps a lid on outrage over the crime of black and Latino children being poorly educated. The consequences of this refusal to speak out are tearing up black America—especially young men searching for identity and direction. Statistics show that 65 percent of black boys who dropped out of high school were unemployed, had stopped looking for work, or were in jail during the year 2000. By 2004, the *New York Times* reported, 72 percent of black men who dropped out of high school were unemployed, no longer looking for work, or behind bars. Half of the black men who dropped out of college were unemployed, too. "Terrible schools, absent parents, racism, the decline in blue collar jobs and a subculture that glorifies swagger over work have all been cited as causes of the deepening ruin of black youth," the *Times* reported in a March 2006 article.

Much of what Cosby is saying is intended to get black leaders to take action on this very agenda. His emphasis on the idea of personal responsibility and accountability is a natural extension of these priorities because it calls out to parents as well as students to take action now to save themselves.

Speaking at the *Brown* anniversary celebration, Cosby said, "In the neighborhoods most of us grew up in, parenting is not going on. In the old days you couldn't play hookey because every drawn shade was an eye. And before your mother got off the bus and to the house she knew exactly where you had gone, who had gone into [your] house . . . parents don't know that today."

Speaking in a lengthy interview for this book, Cosby said that the sense of a community watching over a child also conveyed the demands of the larger society. "Even if it takes a village to raise a child, the village has rules," he said.

Again Cosby put in plain language a reality that experts see in numbers. The problem is not just in teaching or in the educational establishment. It's also a problem of parenting. The gap between black and white students already exists when the children are entering kindergarten. According to the National Center for Education Statistics, half of black children starting kindergarten scored in the bottom quarter on general knowledge; 40 percent of black kindergartners were in the bottom quarter on math; and one-third of black kindergartners were in the bottom quarter on reading. These gaps precede the gulf between black and white students in test scores and high school graduation rates.

Before their first day of school, black children are struggling and falling behind intellectually. At the *Brown* celebration, Cosby called out parents who are willing to buy the latest sneakers and jackets for their preschool children but refuse to spend money on a reading program like Hooked on Phonics. A few months later in Milwaukee, where only 27 percent of black children graduate from high school, Cosby begged black parents to be serious about education from the day a black child is born. "You're not talking to these children . . . stop cursing at your children and grabbing them by the arm," he said. A year later, again in Milwaukee, Cosby heard Bonnie Edwards, a sixty-two-year-old mother of seven grown children who is now raising seven grandchildren, nieces, and nephews, complain that her youngsters are rude, refuse to do chores, and hang out in the street. With some of her grandkids sitting there, she wanted Cosby to blast the children, to tell them to behave. Instead, he blasted her.

"How dare you stand up here and claim that you've been abused when you're abusing yourself," he said. "You let those kids look at you like 'Do it for me!' Who's raising who here? You got to set the rules. [The children] are waiting for you to do that."

In other appearances, Cosby reminded black fathers that "a child who doesn't know his father feels rejected. . . . I don't care if you don't have a job, go by and see your children. Don't let other people raise your children."

Do not think that Cosby is letting black children off the hook. At an event in Richmond, he told students, "Study. That's all. It's not that tough. You're not picking cotton. You're not picking up the trash. You're not washing windows. You sit down. You read. You develop your brain."

There is no getting away, however, from the fact that most of Cosby's fire is aimed at negligent black parents. At one stop he told parents, "We are letting TV sets raise our children." He is exactly right. In a nation where only 37 percent of black children live with a mother and father in two-parent families, there is a real issue of black children, especially the poor, getting little individual attention from parents. Too often in black families, especially single-parent black families, the television set is left to do the parenting.

One recent study found that about 50 percent of black fourth graders watch TV for five or more hours on a typical school day. Fewer than 20 percent of white fourth graders watch that much TV. By the eighth grade, the TV is still dominating the time of young black people. About 45 percent of black eighth graders watch five hours or more of TV on a school day, while fewer than 15 percent of white students are mesmerized by the tube for that long. Of course, this has an impact on study time.

A 1990 study found that black students who said they worked hard to get ahead in school did about four hours of homework a week. White students who felt they were working hard put in about five-and-a-half hours, and Asian American students put in about seven-and-a-half hours, almost twice as much homework time as black students. And yet black parents are not turning off the set and telling their children to hit the books. In fact, when one researcher asked black and Hispanic children what was the lowest grade they could get in school without angering their parents, the answer was C-minus. When the same question was asked of white students, the threshold for facing an angry parent was B-minus. Teachers, especially white teachers, are often criticized for having low expectations of black students, but, sad to say, those low expectations start with black parents.

Incredibly, civil rights leaders have not focused on the message that by turning off the TV, by demanding good grades, and by going into the classroom to work with the teachers, black families have the power to improve the education their children get from big-city schools. Black leadership prefers to put the focus on calls to increase spending for education in big cities. They are at their best when pointing out increasing racial segregation in America's schools, citing statistics that show the schools to be as segregated as they were in 1968. Note that both the complaint about spending and the concern about segregation are outside the power of black parents. And also note that both arguments have their weaknesses.

The spending argument is shaky because in cities like Washington, D.C., the school system fails despite spending more money per pupil than world-class public schools in neighboring suburbs. For example, a 2002 study showed that per-pupil spending in 65 percent of big-city school districts, which have the highest minority student populations, is higher than the average per-pupil spending in the rest of their state.

They have a better argument when it comes to school segregation. There is no doubt about the increasing isolation of black and Latino children in public schools. One-third of black and Hispanic children go to schools that are called "hyper-segregated" because their student body is less than 10 percent white in a nation where over 60 percent of the schoolchildren are white. A typical black or Hispanic student attends a public school that is over two-thirds black and Hispanic, while the typical white student goes to a school that is about 80 percent white. Poverty is also an issue. The big-city schools also have a concentration of poor minority children.

This segregation carries a real cost. With more poverty and more single-parent families among minority students, there is more need for academic support from teachers and aides, as well as for free lunches. There are also more disciplinary issues that disrupt academic study. Those differences are magnified by school segregation. It is most severe for the best black students; their grades and test scores show a big improvement in racially mixed schools, according to recent studies. Studies show a general improvement in test scores for all black and Hispanic students attending more-integrated schools.

But in the current racial climate it is unlikely that even the loudest complaints are going to increase school integration. There is no incentive for white or middle-class minority parents to put their children in struggling big-city schools with large populations of minority students. Even the black middle class is trying to get out. Already, one-third of black middle-class families live in suburbs, and their numbers are growing. Meanwhile, the federal courts are pulling desegregation plans. Busing black students is unpopular with growing numbers of black parents who want neighborhood schools and believe that a black child can get a quality education without sitting next to a white child. It is also a statistical fact that in integrated schools, black and Hispanic students still do not perform as well as white students. Ironically, even middle-class black and Hispanic students in well-funded, integrated schools trail white students in terms of grades and test scores.

The most famous example comes from Shaker Heights, Ohio, where a black researcher, John Ogbu, was invited by black parents in 1997 to help them understand why their children, black students in that school district's middle-class, integrated suburban schools still lagged behind white students on every measure of academic progress. Black students in Shaker Heights had a 1.9 grade point average, as compared with 3.45 for white students.

Ogbu and a research team from the University of California at Berkeley spent nine months looking at test scores and interviewing parents, teachers, and students in that well-to-do suburb with its properly funded, integrated schools and a high level of teachers and support staff. In Shaker Heights, 1990 data showed half of white households and one-third of black households had an income of more than $50,000.

One of Ogbu's most troubling findings is that middle-class black parents spend less time than middle-class white parents in helping their children with homework and staying in touch with teachers. By his measure, middle-class black parents put as little effort into tracking their child's schoolwork as did the poorest white parents. As a result, Ogbu found that from kindergarten to high school, black students put relatively little effort into their schoolwork. In fact, their level of effort went down steadily as they moved from elementary school to high school. They said schoolwork came after TV, sports, talking on the phone, and holding a job. And some black students told him "it was not cool to be successful."

"What amazed me is that these kids who come from homes of doctors and lawyers are not thinking like their parents; they don't know how their parents made it," Ogbu later told the *New York Times*. "They are looking at rappers in ghettos as their role models. . . . The parents work two, three jobs to give their children everything, but they are not guiding their children."

Professor Ogbu sounds a lot like Cosby. His analysis, like Cosby's, attracted hostile critics. And, like Cosby's critics, Ogbu's critics had no evidence to mount a legitimate challenge to the credibility of his work.

That didn't stop the bad-mouthing. The National Urban League put out a statement charging the professor with blaming "the victims of racism." One parent, speaking on a television show, called him an "academic Clarence Thomas." That parent, Khalid Samad, said the black students in Shaker Heights had problems because "the system has de-educated and miseducated African Americans." He said poor schoolwork by black students was a result of their continuing struggles with black identity because of slavery. Another critic, an academic, said Ogbu's data was good, but argued that Ogbu was wrong to think that black students didn't value education just because black students didn't hit the books as hard as white students. In other words, don't judge black students by their actions or performance. Don't look at low grades and lower test scores because even if the students are middle-class, they are black. The excuses piled higher and higher, almost as high as the personal attacks on Ogbu. He was charged with being an African immigrant who did not understand black Americans, and he was also found guilty of underestimating the damage done by a history of discrimination and ongoing racism.

Once again we see the pattern of patronizing black people by giving them power only as victims. Underlying the critics' arguments is the bizarre idea that if black people compete and succeed, then they are not black. And anyone who says that black people can take personal responsibility for making the best of any school is blaming the poor.

This argument takes shape in current politics around President

Bush's policy of testing children for basic skills in English and math every year between the third and eighth grades as well as before they graduate from high school. Schools also have to report on the test scores of minority students to make sure that their problems are not being hidden in overall scores that are bolstered by the performance of white children. The president's plan, called "No Child Left Behind," allows parents to take their children out of schools that fail to raise test scores. The plan has been a target of teachers' unions, which complain that it forces teachers to teach children only how to take tests. There have been complaints, too, that the plan will discourage minority children who don't pass their tests and make them more likely to drop out of school.

The excuses never stop. In this case, however, they have the value of revealing the source of a heavy layer of lies. The big lie is coming from civil rights leaders, Democratic politicians, and the teachers' unions that have been silent about the lack of education in big-city schools, but who are now vocal in their opposition to the president's plan because of concern for black and minority children. The truth is, they don't like any plan that exposes how badly big-city schools perform. Poor black parents want good schools and favor the right to move out of schools that are not teaching their children. That is why parents of poor children tell pollsters they want vouchers, no matter how small, if it means they have a chance to put their child in a better public school or move their child to a parochial or private school.

Superintendents and principals are being forced to pay attention to the achievement gap between black and white students because they have to get test scores up for all students in order to stay in business. Under the alliance between the civil rights leaders and the teachers' unions, the key political concern has been about creating teaching jobs, protecting those jobs, and increasing funding for schools, including money to pay teachers better salaries. What was happening to the students took a back seat. At best, the educational problems of black children offered the union leaders and civil rights leaders the use of a sad child's face as justification for their requests for more money to keep a corrupt system afloat.

The silence from black leaders about the problems of big-city schools stems directly from this political deal. The problem is that this crisis goes far beyond political posturing over budget fights. Real people—children—are being hurt. Even if they can't read, those children are smart enough to know they are being treated like deadwood, warehoused in bad schools where they are told they'll be promoted to the next grade as long as they don't do drugs, fight, or bring guns to school. Any rational person, even the most trusting child, has to feel alienated from a system that is so heartless.

And adults, black and white, who deal with the children coming out of these big-city schools know the young people are not ready to compete at the best colleges. They are not ready to hold jobs that will give them a chance at the middle-class dream. Instead, poor minority children are fed a popular culture full of negative stereotypes that invite them to dismiss school as a waste of time.

The silence from black leaders is evidence of the power of this massive conspiracy. A year after Cosby broke the silence, more voices insisted on speaking out. Brent Staples, an editorial writer for the *New York Times*, wrote that while the civil rights movement is "fearful of taking positions that would discomfort the teachers among its supporters," it is a crime for anyone who cares about poor children to "stand on the sidelines." Staples wrote:

"Unless the civil rights establishment adopts a stronger and more public position it will inevitably be viewed as having missed the most important civil rights battle of the last half-century."

The same message came from columnist Joseph H. Brown in the *Tampa Tribune*, when he wrote that the achievement gap between black and white children has less to do with school funding or racially biased tests than it does with silence that encourages the "cultural belief [among young people] that being 'authentically black' does not allow for high quality intellectual engagement in school." Breaking that silence, he added, requires a "new movement devoted to the cause of educational excellence with the same dedication as the one for civil rights." Brown quoted an elderly black resident of Tampa who had been a civil rights leader in the 1950s and 1960s, during the time of the *Brown* decision, as once hearing from the mayor of Tampa that the city needed black police officers, but could not find qualified applicants. At the time, the civil rights leader Bob Gilder raised his voice in the black community to say, "We've engaged in sit-ins, wade-ins, and walk-ins. I suggest we engage in some study-ins."

That is the brand of courage that is needed right now from black leaders nationwide. It is a willingness to speak truth inside the black community. It is a willingness to pay the price for speaking in defiance of political alliances and deals that have left black children wandering like lost souls in a biblical desert, subject to all sorts of illusions and distortions that twist centuries of efforts by black people to educate themselves and their children into the illusion that educated black people are acting white.

This is the brand of courage that Bill Cosby displayed at the *Brown* gala. It is the courage he showed when he later wrote that there is no need for any more panels or commissions to study the problem of the achievement gap or bad schools in minority neighborhoods. "What we need now," Cosby wrote in a column in the *Los Angeles Times*, "is parents sitting down with children, overseeing homework, sending children off to school in the morning, well-fed, clothed, rested, and ready to learn . . . change can only be set in motion when families and leaders get together and acknowledge that a problem exists. Where are the standards that tell a child: 'Stop! There is hope.' This has to happen in the home. It reverts back to parenting."

That is a call to arms for black people to stop waiting for the end of "systemic racism" or for more money for schools. A black child born today will be old or dead long before the end of racism or before a time when every public school is successfully reformed. America is now at the point where giving hope to black children is a radical idea. It is radical to speak against an anti-educational mindset and in favor of reclaiming the black heritage of making education the heart of the struggle for racial equality. The key is breaking the silence. As it says in the Bible, "In the beginning was the Word." Cosby offered such a word when he reminded black parents that in 1957 black children had to endure violence from mobs, "being hit in the face with rocks and punched in the face" to get into Little Rock's Central High School. Cosby was trying to shock people into action when he spoke of that heroic sacrifice and then contrasted it to so many black children standing outside schools today, cursing, fighting, and dressing like thugs.

To repeat the message addressed to black America: "What the hell good is *Brown v. Board of Education* if nobody wants it?"

5

CRIME AND PUNISHMENT

A FEW DAYS AFTER his controversial speech in Washington, Bill Cosby made headlines again. This time he broke the taboo against prominent black voices speaking out about African Americans and crime.

"You've got to stop beating up your women because you can't find a job, because you didn't want to get an education and now you're [earning] minimum wage," Cosby said. Then he listed the violence and threats faced by civil rights workers during the 1950s and 1960s to win the *Brown* decision, the Civil Rights Act, and the Voting Rights Act. And he mentioned Emmett Till, the fourteen-year-old killed in Mississippi by white racists for simply talking to a white woman, as another example of what black people have overcome to open doors for this generation of black Americans. "Dogs, water hoses that tear the bark off trees, Emmett Till. And you're going to tell me that you're going to drop out of school? You're going to tell me that you are going to steal from a store?"

Very few leading black voices in the pulpit or on the political stage are focused on having black people take personal responsibility for the exorbitant amount of crime committed by black people against other black people. Today's black leaders sing like a choir when they raise their voices against police brutality and the increasing number of black people in jail. The high note is always centered on white politicians who demonize black criminals. There are complaints about legislators who get headlines by increasing jail sentences and calling it a "War on Drugs," as more people, disproportionately black and Hispanic, end up in jail for longer periods. There are complaints about the ever-expanding "Prison Industrial Complex," which requires more prisoners to create more jobs for construction workers, guards, and every other sector that earns dollars from a captive population. And judges who treat small-time drug dealers and addicts as major criminals also get blasted by the choir as part of a regularly repeated litany. Lashing out at racism in the criminal justice system is on the front page of the black leadership songbook—and not without justification. But any mention of black America's responsibility for committing the crimes, big and small, that lead so many to prison is barely mumbled if mentioned at all.

Cosby first broke with this orthodoxy during his original speech in May, but his barbed comments about crime might have been overlooked because they were so far out of the box. Cosby dumped the official script when he cursed the stupidity of black thieves, drug dealers, and stickup artists. He really went off message when he directed fury at the parents, the church leaders, and the black intellectuals who defend black criminals as victims of racism deserving of sympathy. Cosby had another idea. He said they deserved contempt. He called them pure thugs, knuckle-heads, and an embarrassment to the race.

"Look at the incarcerated [population of black people, especially black men], these people are not political [prisoners]," Cosby said, raising his voice to a yell. It was the one time during the Washington speech when he seemed almost out of emotional control. The spirit clearly moved him on this topic.

"These people are going around stealing Coca-Cola. People getting shot in the back of the head over a piece of pound cake! Then we all run out and are outraged [saying], 'The cops shouldn't have shot him.' What the hell was he doing with the pound cake in his hand?" Applause filled Constitution Hall. The people hearing Cosby must have agreed, and wanted their official black leaders to listen to him.

Cosby tied the high rate of black inmates to what he described as criminally bad parenting, mothers and fathers failing to spend time with their children, especially men who don't stay around after they get a woman pregnant. "I'm talking about these people who cry when their son is standing there in an orange suit [the standard outfit given to prisoners once their clothes are taken away]. Where were you when he was two? Where were you when he was twelve [or] eighteen and how come you didn't know he had a pistol?"

And he asked why black families were not insisting that black churches get out front, using the pulpit to point out the horror of crimes being committed by black people against black people in black neighborhoods. "Christians, what's wrong with you? Why can't you hit the streets? Why can't you clean it out yourselves?" he asked, after saying that the Black Muslims know how to clear a neighborhood of drug dealers and thieves.

And he didn't stop there. He kept coming back to the issue of black crime throughout his speech, and he made a direct connection between the high crime rate in black neighborhoods and the failure of so many people to take personal responsibility for getting an education.

"These people are fighting hard to be ignorant. There's no English being spoken, and they're walking and they're angry," Cosby said, pointing to the 50-percent black dropout rate and a culture that allows five generations to live in a housing project with no sense of shame. "Oh God, they're angry and they have pistols and they shoot and they do stupid things. And after they kill somebody, they don't have a plan. Just murder somebody. Boom. Over what? A pizza?"

At a later town-hall meeting in Detroit, Cosby used his talent as a comedian to mock black leaders who excuse the high black crime rate as part of "systemic" racism. Acting the part of an indignant black leader, he complained that the "system" and "the man" give longer jail sentences to poor black people for smoking crack cocaine than to rich white people for snorting more-expensive powdered cocaine. What would happen if white and black cocaine dealers got the same sentence, he asked.

"Okay, we even it up, let's have a big cheer for the white man doing as much time as the black man. Hooray!" said Cosby. "Anybody see any sense in this? Systemic racism they call it." Then he burst out of his parody and said it straight: Why don't black leaders, black parents, black church people and schoolteachers, tell these black children to stop selling crack cocaine? Why don't more black leaders point out that crack devastates black people, hurts black families, and spreads crime in black neighborhoods? Why didn't a single leader crusade as a crime fighter in the name of revitalizing black neighborhoods by allowing businesses and families to take root in a safe, drug-free black neighborhood?

The silence on the subject of black crime is mind-boggling. The statistics on black crime are screaming for attention and debate. To be blunt, black criminals are a crushing burden weighing down black people. They represent a regressive force that gives credence to the racist stereotype of black people, especially young black men, as a race of marauding, jobless thugs. This was the libel used against freed slaves after the Civil War, as in the Klan-lionizing film *Birth of a Nation*. That piece of propaganda justified racism as a necessary defense against a predatory, primitive, sex-crazed black people unleashed from social control with the end of slavery. By that logic, criminal activity by blacks required decent white people to band together against lawless blacks in the name of decency and public safety. It also led to a "convict lease" system that sent former slaves to jail in massive numbers for trumped-up crimes, where they could once again be forced to work without being paid. Encouraging fear of all blacks as rapists and murderers also led to the spread of "strange fruit," black people dangling from trees at the end of a hangman's noose. The horror of lynching was principally justified by Southern politicians as necessary to show that white people had the ability and the right to protect themselves against black criminals.

The destructive power of black crime at the end of the twentieth century was laid bare in a widely reported comment made by Jesse Jackson in 1993. As the unchallenged leader in black America after his two presidential campaigns, an unscripted Jackson said, "There is nothing more painful to me at this stage in my life than to walk down the street and hear footsteps and start thinking about robbery and then look around and see somebody white and feel relieved." That quote from Mr. Black America stripped naked the torment in the black community over black-on-black crime. It was a shock that Jackson was so honest and for people outside the black community it was also proof that, even the celebrated Jesse Jackson, lived in fear of being a crime victim at the hands of black people.

The white racist stereotype of all blacks as criminals is nothing compared to black people living with a sense of an enemy within. That enemy is a neighbor, a friend, possibly a child, any of whom is capable of robbing and assaulting them. Jackson's comment was an admission of the unsettling, undeniable fact that so much crime against black people comes from black hands. Bill

Cosby, talking about the same problem in an interview for this book, recounted seeing black boys strutting, shouting, and cursing as they walked through a mall. "Young black people getting off frightening old white people," he said. "They don't know they are frightening their own people. Every day, less and less, you have people who [don't] want anything to do with them."

In October 2002 the living hell caused by crime in the black community burst into flames in Baltimore.

A black mother of five testified against a Northeast Baltimore drug dealer. The next day her row house was fire-bombed. She managed to put out the flames that time. Two weeks later, at 2:00 a.m. as the family slept, the house was set on fire again. This time the drug dealer broke open the front door and took care in splashing gasoline on the lone staircase that provided exit for people asleep in the second- and third-floor bedrooms. Angela Dawson, the thirty-six-year-old mother, and her five children, aged nine to fourteen, burned to death. Her husband, Carnell, forty-three, jumped from a second-story window. He had burns over most of his body and died a few days later. On that chilling night, as she struggled against the smoke and heat, the mother's cries could be heard over the crackle of the flames on East Preston Street. "God, please help me," screamed Angela Dawson. "Help me get my children out."

Before she was silenced, Dawson made thirty-six calls to the police, from late July until her death, to complain about the drug dealers who operated freely on the street in front of her house. About a month before she was killed, one of the dealers had scrawled BITCH on the front wall of her house. As she was scrubbing away the graffiti, a young man who lived across the street, an eighteen-year-old, appeared and boldly said he had written the word there, told her to leave it alone, and then hit her.

The teenager who slugged her, John L. Henry, was charged

with assault. He was already on probation for carrying a gun. But after a brief court hearing, he was sent home, and the very next day two bottles of burning gasoline came crashing through the Dawsons' kitchen window. Then, two weeks later, the blaze was set that burned down the house and killed the family. The man charged with setting the fatal blaze lived next door to Henry.

The murderer was Darrell Brooks, twenty-one, a convicted car thief known in the neighborhood for criminal activity with the "283 Crew." The gang spray-painted vacant buildings where they did drug business with the letters RIP. Police later described Brooks as a small-time drug trafficker who sold heroin and crack. As part of a plea deal to avoid the death penalty, he confessed to having set the earlier fire that burned the Dawson house. According to police records, Brooks had told other young men in the drug trade in East Baltimore before the first fire that he planned to burn the family out because "Mrs. Dawson is snitching on people." Brooks pleaded guilty to the crime of killing the five children and two adults in exchange for a sentence of life in jail without parole.

One neighbor, David Parker, told the *Baltimore Sun:* "These drug dealers have it set up around here that people are scared to speak up because of what they will do if you try to disrupt their drug trade. They got it so if you speak up, you will be dealt with. When night falls around here, the older people don't come out and you can't blame them. Half the time you can't even walk down the street." Neighborhood leaders explained that in the East Oliver section of the city, it makes sense to keep quiet and let the drug lords run the show. In some cases the drug dealers hand out a little cash or free samples. At that point everyone is in on the conspiracy. A year earlier, one of Dawson's neighbors dared to open her mouth and tell local drug runners to stop using her back alley as a stash. She had a bottle broken over her head and was left bloody. Her minister organized a one-time march of two hundred people from Memorial Baptist Church to show support for her. But constant late-night threats increased, and she fled the neighborhood. As the newspaper reported: "Families [here] are often unwilling to join the battle against crime because it would mean turning in a child, grandchild, cousin, or uncle. . . . Residents still may have to coexist with neighbors who might be criminals."

The extreme act of killing an entire family led Baltimore politicians to call Angela Dawson "the Rosa Parks of the Drug War." The White House drug czar said the family had fought the drug dealers in the spirit of the biblical hero Daniel, a man who refused to bow down before false gods. Neighbors put teddy bears on the steps of the burned-out house in tribute to the children who died. Someone put out a plastic jar, and money was collected for the family's burial. Someone else put up a poster, next to the teddy bears and a few balloons. It read, THINK OF THE CHILDREN—STOP THE MADNESS!

Yet the madness goes on. Drug abuse and gangs warring over drug money is everyday business in too many black neighborhoods. So, too, is the corruption of using young people to carry and sell drugs. And today a "stop snitching" movement grows, further intimidating people in the community looking for police protection, while encouraging neighbors to take a blind eye to the breakdown of their own communities. That movement is being led by drug dealers, but it has found support among academics. For example, Alexandra Natapoff, an associate law professor at Loyola Law School, argues that cooperating with the police, including criminals "snitching" on one another to get lower sentences, is bad for black neighborhoods. The professor writes that "snitching exacerbates crime, violence, and distrust in some of the nation's most socially vulnerable communities." Once again, there is no clear statement that selling drugs, mugging people, shooting and killing rivals, and robbing stores is wrong and destroys black communities.

That had been the case in East Baltimore for more than a decade before the Dawson family died. One of the first times Angela Dawson took the risk of talking to the police about the drug dealers, a brick was thrown through one of her home's windows, and glass fragments got into one child's eye. Mrs. Dawson filed a compliant to the police. She said she saw the man who threw the brick and screamed for help as he ran away. But, she wrote in the complaint, "most of the people who were sitting on the streets were [the suspect's] family and friends." They refused to help her. The hear-no-evil, see-no-evil neighbors had become silent partners in the conspiracy that eventually killed the Dawson family. Yet no civil rights leaders, no ministers, and no politicians had anything to say until drug dealers went all the way and killed the Dawson family.

Black crime is a cancer that is quietly killing the moral center of black America. The strongest argument from Dr. King and the entire civil rights movement was always a call for equal rights as a matter of justice under law and Judeo-Christian morality. That call for racial justice loses its power when it comes from people with dirty hands. Fear of crime committed by black people inflames negative feelings about black people in the white community. Even worse, the growth of black crime forces black people to deny and excuse the corruption in their midst. When anyone mentions the prevalence of crime in black neighborhoods and its casual acceptance by so many black people, heads turn the other way. Standing up to the issue requires black leaders to condemn black criminals as sellouts who betray a long tradition of black people taking a stand for brotherhood, promoting positive, strong images of black life and community.

In an interview for this book, Bill Cosby noted that the NAACP's national headquarters is located in Baltimore, a city with one of the highest murder rates in the nation. "I've never once heard the NAACP say, 'Let's do something about this,'" said Cosby. They never marched or organized, or even criticized the criminals.

Unfortunately, no black leader during the 1990s dared to go after black criminals, with the exception of Louis Farrakhan. His Nation of Islam found a lucrative business as crime-fighters. Farrakhan traded on the Nation's reputation for recruiting former hardened convicts, experienced criminals, to protect black people against the criminals in their midst.

Apart from Farrakhan, civil rights and black church leaders pointed a finger at white cops, prosecutors, judges, and jailers as the source of the black crime problem. They said the increase in incarcerated black people was largely the result of an unfair increase in sentences for drug possession and drug dealing as part of the late-1970s and early-1980s "war on drugs." It is true that the "war on drugs" was a political craze, a mania requiring everyone to lie about the huge appetite for drugs in all parts of America— rich, poor, black, white, urban and suburban—and ignored the need for rehabilitation.

The lack of balance in dealing with drug use was a small point, however, when compared with the horrific reality of war zones created by dealers and addicts in black America. Black people, especially working-class black people, were under siege, with bars on their windows and alarms on their cars, to guard against an epidemic of crack addicts and gun-happy crack dealers. Retail businesses, from restaurants to newsstands, fled black neighborhoods. The black middle class, even the lower middle class, followed the track that whites had cut from the city to the suburbs.

Yet crime and its devastating consequences for urban black neigh-borhoods nationwide were ignored by black leaders. Instead of speaking out against gangs, drug dealers, and pimps—and the clothes and hip-hop music that celebrated these outlaws as black heroes—left-wing intellectuals preached against the sins of the white racist American establishment. They particularly blamed the police for the rising numbers of blacks in jail. They asked why white people who used drugs in their suburban homes, on college campuses, and in downtown office towers, did not get arrested at the same rate as black people. The fashionable theory was that America's poor, disproportionately black and concentrated in big cities, did their drug deals and robberies on street corners where lazy, racist police had an easy time arresting them.

Never a word was spoken about the need for black Americans to take up their own war on drugs and on crime as a matter of personal responsibility. And no one testified that crime by black hands undercut the advances in racial justice and the opportuni-ties opened up by the great civil rights movement.

All the silence could not blind anyone to the neon lights flash-ing sad facts about the severity of black crime. By 2004 federal data showed that black Americans—13 percent of the popula-tion—accounted for 37 percent of the violent crimes, 54 percent of arrests for robbery, and 51 percent of murders. Most of the vic-tims of these violent criminals were their fellow black people. This legitimate fear of violent crime by black people spread into every corner of the nation, thanks to the success of law-and-order appeals from politicians. White, conservative politicians realized they had a winning formula for any campaign by simply playing to white suburban anxiety about violent black criminals in the city. The politicians didn't have to call names and point at black people; it was enough to talk about crime. Any mention of violent crime automatically brought black people to the minds of America's overwhelmingly white voters.

The face of crime became a black man's face. It was Willie Horton, a convicted rapist, whose scary face was used to pump up votes for George H. W. Bush's presidential campaign in 1988. Black rappers also did their part to promote black identity as the criminals' identity. Black rappers dressed for every video in convict style, posturing with menacing faces, hands flashing gang signals, their heads wrapped in prison-issue do-rags, pants hanging down in the convict style, and gangland tattoos covering their bodies.

The intersection of race and crime has forced American politics to make some deals. The most obvious deal is having black people put on the uniform of top police officials, if not the police chief, in major cities. There has been a similar push to increase the number of black judges who are sending black people to jail. But the judges are generally hidden inside courtrooms. The police chiefs become the face of law enforcement on the nightly news.

Why are so many police chiefs black? Obviously it gives politicians, black and white, immediate cover against charges of police brutality and misconduct in dealing with black criminals. It is hard to make men such as Lee Brown and Richard Pennington into Mark Fuhrman or Bull Connor. Today that means no mayor, black or white, wants to have a Fuhrman or a Bull Connor speaking for the city government if there is trouble between black people and the police. The mayors understand the utility of having an attractive black police chief to handle the two most common complaints about police: misconduct by officers (such as the cruel beating of Rodney King) or charges that police are inattentive to crime in black neighborhoods.

The best police chiefs are the people who can negotiate the tension inside the black community over policing. On one side are black people who fear the police, and on the other are black people who need the police to protect them. Often, fear of the police and need for the police live in a single mind.

What is the single solution to both problems, fear of police and fear of crime? These are not contradictory issues. Why would any local black leader want to see more black people under arrest—his neighbors, their sons and daughters? Why wouldn't any local black leader want to create a safe community for his neighbors, sons, and daughters?

The solution requires an honest commitment from black leadership to say that the black criminal is no friend of black progress. By reducing black crime, both fear of the police and fear of crime will diminish. This doesn't let racist cops off the hook, but it does allow us, to the degree it is under our control, to lessen the impact of both bad policing and the threat of crime.

In 2005, when William Bennett, the former federal drug czar, said that the crime rate in America could be reduced if all black babies were aborted, there was a storm of criticism, and for good reason. It was an indefensible comment, with genocidal overtones. Bennett's unprompted mention of this explosive theory on his radio show left him little ground for defense against charges of racism. He talked as if crime and blackness were genetically linked. Even if he was only talking about poor black people, as opposed to all black people, and the relatively high rate of poor black Americans involved with crime, Bennett might have considered the implications of similar attempts at social engineering by abortion. Is he willing to kill off white babies, on the basis of statistics, to reduce the corporate crime rate or the number of mass murderers? Bennett's remarks were clearly insane.

The comments did prompt rational arguments about the impact of poverty and unemployment on the crime rate. Bennett's supporters rightly pointed to the simple fact that statistics show black Americans to be responsible for a disproportionate share of the crimes committed in the United States. And even Bennett's critics know that America's prisons are filled with black faces.

Black people make up 13 percent of the nation's population, but in 2003 the nation's prison population was 44 percent black, according to the U.S. Justice Department. One of every ten black men between the ages of twenty-five and twenty-nine is in prison. There has been a steady increase in the black jail population since 1995, when a report from the Sentencing Project (a Washington, D.C.–based group that does legal research on the criminal justice system) found that one-third of all black American men, aged twenty to twenty-nine, were on any given day in jail or prison, on probation or on parole. The report said that more black men were in jail or prison than in college. A black male child born in 2001 has a 33-percent chance of going to prison at some point in his life, according to the study.

Oddly, the increase in the black prison population begins around the time of the 1954 *Brown* decision. At the start of the 1950s, 65 percent of all state and federal prisoners were white and 35 percent were black. At that midcentury point, poverty, bad housing, racist cops, legal discrimination, and high unemployment all were cited as the reasons that the percentage of black people in prison was more than triple the percentage of black people in the nation. By the end of the century the percentage of white prisoners had declined to 35 percent, while the black inmate population approached 50 percent. Something terrible had happened.

Part of that terrible something was crack cocaine. Turf fights between gangs of dealers in big cities made drive-by shootings a regular and frightful feature of the urban landscape. And crack addicts, desperate for their next hit, pumped up the number of muggings, break-ins, and stickups. Crack houses sprang up in working-class neighborhoods, driving away the last middle-class families and creating urban war zones dominated by criminals and an economy based on crime and illegal drug sales. The well-worn argument that "systemic" racism was putting all these black people in jail was being crushed by the reality of genuine fear that people of every color and class felt from black crime, especially violent black crime like drive-by shootings and murderous corner-store robberies.

Nightly local news programs and TV shows like *Cops* drew big ratings by playing on the fear of urban black criminals. According to the Sentencing Project, between 1986 and 1991, as crack became an epidemic in big cities, there was a 465-percent increase in the number of black people behind bars. Fear of addicts on crime sprees led judges to set longer prison sentences and politicians to demand life sentences after three convictions (three strikes and you're out), as well as mandatory minimum sentences. Even after crime began going down in 1992, the new laws remained in place and continued to drop the hammer on people caught for any criminal activity, which included a large number of black people.

The harsh sentencing rules are unfair and need to be changed, yes, but, as Cosby pointed out, "what the hell was he doing with the pound cake in his hand?" Making excuses for black criminals amounts to a deal with the devil for black families and black neighborhoods. First, a criminal adds no value to the community. He or she is robbing literal valuables from a community, and is also ripping away the sense of safety that is critical to every human life. Second, a criminal, in or out of jail, is not investing in the neighborhood by working a job, taking care of children, offering a model of independence or political involvement. The loss of the right to vote for so many black people, as a price for being a convicted felon, also hurts the political power of the black community. Obviously a criminal is also not a good choice for a spouse, a parent, or an elected official.

Yet somehow the stigma of being a criminal vanishes when excuses are made and it becomes so commonplace for young black men to be under arrest, in jail, and on probation. In some neighborhoods the stigma even gets turned on its head. Going to jail becomes a rite of passage for a young male to prove himself. The emergence of the black gangster as a common hero in music and movies is more poison being injected into young black minds. Here is an open sewer throwing up the idea that black men are most genuine, most in touch with their power, when they are getting vengeance with a gun in hand. Yet no leader says anything. One statistical model in the 1990s put the likelihood of a low-income black man going to prison during his lifetime at 60 percent. And remember that any black male—rich or poor—born in 2001 had a 33-percent chance of ending up in jail. Now add to this that the average sentence for an inmate is two and a half years, with most finding themselves back behind bars within three years of release, and you can see the depth of the damage to individuals, families, communities, and the black nation. This is a criminal waste of minds and life, and it is a rebuke to the black tradition of beating the odds to achieve and offer the next generation a boost toward equality.

Also, many criminals create a cycle of self-defeat for themselves. In jail they learned the skills, the mindset, and the connections for a lifetime of criminal activity. At the end of 2003, 10 percent of all black men between the ages of twenty-five and twenty-nine—the time for young adults to establish a foundation of skills, career development, and job networks—could be found in prison. A criminal record also makes it harder to get a job, and for a poor black man, getting a job is already a challenge. Given this awful reality, it makes sense for black mothers, fathers, ministers, teachers, coaches, and friends to rage against criminal activity. The heartfelt message from all caring adults to any young black man or woman can be powerful in its simplicity and truth: Use any means necessary to stay out of this net of crime, police, and prison. It is a highway to a life of hell. And the message has to be delivered early—as a warning, yes, but even more as an encouragement about the child's power to achieve greatness through education and hard work.

Parents also have the chance to be role models for children by not being criminals, including using crime as a justification for keeping guns in the house or carrying guns on the street. Census statistics indicate that nearly 70 percent of black children have single mothers, and estimates are that an even larger percentage will grow up without a regular father in their home. As Cosby said during a visit to Milwaukee, a city with a sky-high murder rate, black children are hurt by the absence of parents and eagerly follow any example of leadership—from gangs to older friends to parents who offer bad examples. So they get a gun, and then, as Cosby described it, "you're asking for trouble . . . you have guns in the hands of people who are already angry because they've been abandoned by a father or mother, or they have lives with very low self-esteem, the anger level is so high."

The explosive mix can be boiled down to absent parents, dropping out of school, and acceptance of criminal behavior that results in jail time. It is a cycle that is reversing the gains of the civil rights movement, including the *Brown* decision.

Cosby picked up on this idea of breaking the cycle of despair in an op-ed piece he wrote in the *Los Angeles Times* in June 2004: "What can the future hold for us with a 50-percent high school dropout rate in many urban areas and with a 60-percent illiteracy rate among inmates and a prison population that is 45 percent black."

The relationship between illiteracy and young black people who end up in the prison system is the key to all Cosby is saying. "Studies show a correlation between inadequate schooling and a wide range of distressing outcomes, including early death, a propensity toward violence and substance abuse," Cosby wrote. "Given the high dropout rate at many urban high schools, it is easy to understand why the social fabric has become tattered." In the days after his first comments about crime at the 2004 *Brown* celebration in Washington, Cosby sent the press a statement in which he explained that he was speaking out as a call to end the feeling of helplessness among black people dealing with crime in the black community. He wanted to ignite "righteous indignation" as a basis for action against this scourge. He was willing to mention this cruel monster in the house as a first step toward organizing a plan for fighting back.

"I travel the country and see these patterns in every community," Cosby said in his statement, "stories of twelve-year-old children killed in the crossfire between knuckleheads selling drugs, the fourteen-year-olds with a sealed envelope as their first step into the criminal justice system."

Once eyes are open to the monstrous impact of crime, the question arises of black families taking personal responsibility for breaking the cycle. And that leads to the question of parents who not only keep guns out of the house, but raise children who understand the idea of personal responsibility and are willing to do the right thing and avoid criminal behavior. After Cosby's speech in Washington, the city's police chief, Charles H. Ramsey, an African American, told him, "I'm with you 100 percent. Behavior has to change. Responsibility for your own behavior has to change. We have people who just let TV and video games and music raise their kids and instill values . . . and then we wonder why we have a problem."

Cosby is speaking hard truths when he sees the answer to many of the black community's problems with crime in personal responsibility. That means not tolerating criminal activity by friends, relatives, and neighbors. That means saying out loud that there is a link between dropouts and criminals. That means drug money is dirty money even if it buys the best. Hard truths are hard to swallow. But unless a hard-line, uncompromising position is taken against crime in the black community, it will remain a major roadblock to improving the chance for all black people, especially poor black people, to take advantage of opportunities that have opened up over the last fifty years.

Here's an idea: Bill Cosby for police chief of Black America.

6

BEATDOWN

ART OF THE GENIUS of black life in America comes down to our ability to make something out of nothing, "a way out of no way," as the saying goes. Black people, cooking with nothing but what was left from the master's table, collards, chitterlings, and pork fat, made a delicious something out of nothing. The black church, with its majestic preaching and powerful singing, was built on a cornerstone of outright rejection: white Christians didn't want black people in their pews. The best example of black Americans finding a way out of no way is black music. The innovators who blazed the trail for black musical forms like gospel, blues, and jazz were men and women with little music education and few instruments, who nevertheless found a way to create a new sound. They used their voices, hands, and feet to make a joyful noise and tell their story.

Rap and its hip-hop beat fits in this glorious tradition. Black New Yorkers literally tapped into the left-over electricity from big-city street lights to power their sound systems and set a thumping beat for their Caribbean-style dance-hall parties on streetcorners and parks. At a time when music education was being cut from city schools, these young souls literally scratched new sounds out of old records. DJs launched a sonic revolution, cutting, scratching, and sampling the best instrumental and vocal riffs on old songs to create a brand new soundscape. Rap, too, came out of nothing. It was just rhyming over the beat. It did not even require a good singing voice. Initially, hip-hop was the lively, deep-bass-and-funky-drum soundtrack for block parties for young black people who were too broke to get into New York's disco clubs. The same spark of creativity and energy from marginalized young people in Ronald Reagan's America led to break dancing: young men and women at clubs and house parties, on the streets and subways, spinning, jumping, and rolling to the beat. The defiant genius of black life is written large over hip-hop.

And like all beauty and new creations, rap and hip-hop were open to corruption. The raw charm of street kids boasting about their ability to rap, to put the most delightful rhymes together, was not immune from the darker forces in urban America. Initially, even as the raps themselves kept to the party spirit of the earliest hip-hop, there were fights, gunfire, and sometimes all-out riots at rap concerts. Over time—especially after the massive success of NWA (Niggaz With Attitude) in the early 1990s—the content of the music became more and more violent. Some of the gritty commentary was improvised reporting from the front lines of the increasingly violent streets of the black inner city during the explosion in violent crime that followed the crack epidemic. But before long the gritty street reporting gave way to nihilistic glorifications of the "thug life." Some of the biggest names in rap, such as Tupac Shakur, swallowed too much of their own poisonous outlaw fantasy and ended up in real-life violent confrontations with real-life consequences: prison, death. Along the same path to corruption, the early hip-hop tradition of young men bragging in their raps about being great, passionate lovers took a wrong turn down a path to degrading women as "whores" and "bitches." Time after time, raising the stakes in rap to get attention from listeners and record companies meant descending to self-hating vulgarity (shout-outs to friends and foes alike meant calling them "nigger" or "motherfucker"). In this toxic punch, the power of good sex turned into crass odes to women showing their genitals ("Pop that pussy, ho . . .") and a bloody tribute to making a woman scream by getting to "gut" her like an animal or "crush" her. The genius of mixing music and poetry to tell the story of struggling against bad schools, tight money, and abusive cops somehow got corrupted into unthinking social commentary like "Face Down, Ass Up, C'mon" and "Fuck the Police."

Major American music companies could not get away with selling rap records that incited attacks on police for long, even when they dressed it up as the voice of protest. Policemen have unions and political support from the White House to city hall.

Black men bragging about their ability to kill other black men— well, that's another story. There was nothing preventing those songs from being recorded and released in massive numbers—except common sense. And common sense was dismissed by rappers and their corporate partners as feeble protests from stuck-up white people and bourgeois black people who had lost touch with their ghetto roots. The defense of gangster rap, with its pride in guns and murder, was that it was all about "keepin' it real." In that stunning perversion of black culture, anyone who spoke against the self-destructive core of gangster rap was put down as acting white or selling out the ghetto. Violence, murder, and self-hatred were marketed as true blackness—authentic black identity.

Similarly, nothing put a brake on the increasingly coarse sex raps, allowing major corporations to make money from the spectacle of young black men acting like the worst racial stereotypes of the unfeeling stud, Mandingo the muscle-bound slave, rutting with black whores. Unfortunately, there is no union of black women with the power to turn up the pressure on corporate America. The White House and city hall have little to say about how black women are denigrated by black men. And just as rappers tagged critics of gangster rap as acting white, any critic of lyrics that denigrated black women was dismissed as a prude or a censor.

And that defense from the rappers has silenced critics and allowed the rappers to keep cashing in for years. But the hateful attacks on black women stoked a few remaining sparks of criticism.

That led to one of the most interesting in-house social confrontations among black Americans so far in the twenty-first century. It is an argument that fits with Bill Cosby's very public challenge to black people, especially the poor, to wise up and turn away from self-defeating behavior that limits their capacity to take advantage of the doors that have opened in the fifty years since the *Brown* decision. Cosby specifically challenged young black women. Talking to a Milwaukee audience about rap music, he asked how many of the women in the audience considered themselves "bitches and hos." When no one raised a hand, a wide-eyed Cosby asked, "If you're not a bitch or a ho, why do you dance to that music?"

Good question.

In his interview for this book, Cosby took an even harder line on hip-hop. He pointed to a conversation with the president of Morgan State University about how young black people dress when they first come to the Baltimore school. The young women dress like prostitutes and the young men come in looking like thugs, Cosby said, as the result of rap filling radio and TV with distorted images of black people that have nothing to do with a history of self-determination and pride. "In order for hip-hop, with all that misogyny and gangster violence and 'don't study,' to exist you've got to know nothing about history, struggle, what it takes to get ahead."

In April 2004 the rapper Nelly had to cancel an appearance at Spelman College in Atlanta when students at the black women's college announced plans for a demonstration against negative images of black women in his raps. There was no arguing the charge. In the video for his rap "Tip Drill" (as in the tip of his penis drilling into a woman), Nelly reduced a black female dancer to a credit-card machine. He literally swiped a credit card between the cheeks of her butt. She responded like a slot machine with a fresh deposit of a quarter. The mindless dancer began to whir, shake, and shimmy her black backside.

The video became a sensation as people talked about its comic and crass content. But for a group of young black women at Spelman, it was "the straw that broke the camel's back." They had been dancing to the beat, even inviting the celebrity rap star to bring his fund-raiser for bone-marrow transplants to their campus. But when the undergrads at Spelman asked Nelly to defend his portrayal of black women, the rapper backed out completely. He canceled the fund-raiser after refusing to join the discussion. Spelman student government president Asha Jennings told the *Atlanta Journal-Constitution:* "We care about the cause [bone marrow transplants], but we can't continue to support artists and images that exploit our women and put us out there as oversexed, unintelligent human beings."

What was astounding about the black women at Spelman challenging Nelly is that it broke a taboo. No group of young black women had ever challenged a rapper for his ugly treatment of black women. In 1993, C. Delores Tucker, a political activist in the National Congress of Black Women, with the quiet support of two prominent black female entertainers, Dionne Warwick and Melba Moore, led a fight to make Time-Warner take responsibility for the violence and woman-hating in videos produced by one of its divisions, Death Row Records. But Tucker was put down as a cranky, old-school black woman long out of touch with the streets. And it didn't help her street credibility that similar complaints about rap had come from establishment white women such as Tipper Gore, the wife of then-senator Al Gore, and Phyllis Schlafly, a conservative activist.

Meanwhile, self-confident, young black women remained lockjaw-silent. In fact, they danced along to the steady rhythm of excuses. They sang along with the rationale that "it's just music"; that it is music for adults who get the joke; and that the videos made big money for black people, and no sane brother or sister should mess with "crazy bank" or "dough on the flow." It was also a fact, the rappers said, that no one forced the girls in the videos to be there, shaking their asses. And, like gangster rap, the pimping of black women in videos was defended as an authentic expression of black life under attack from critics lost in the white world. In other words, the critics simply hated the success of rappers. If the critics were right, the rappers asked where were the smart, happening, young black women complaining about being put down and defiled by rappers? The fact is that for more than a decade no group of young black women emerged to say their public image, their identity, was being trampled by rappers. Young black women were silenced by the same raft of guilt trips, intimidation, and excuses that kept leading voices in black America—before Bill Cosby—from saying out loud that too many black people were hurting themselves with poor parenting and a lack of seriousness about education.

When the women at Spelman stood up to Nelly, they opened a big door to serious discussion of the impact of rappers constantly demeaning black women. *Essence* magazine, self-described as the "world's foremost publication for black women," held a forum at the Atlanta school a few months later under the banner "Take Back the Music."

The magazine had long struggled with rap's putdown of black women as "Bitches" and "Pigeons." Initially it even voiced support for the bad-boy style of the music. In 1999, *Essence* published excerpts from a small group discussion for men only on hip-hop. The introduction by Kevin Powell, a poet and journalist, claimed that any criticism of hip-hop was part of a plot to emasculate black men. "Where else can [black men] verbally flex and not get kicked out of our schools, fired from our jobs, hit upside the head by the police or just outright killed for being our bold, bad-assed selves? From . . . things that repress us—economics, politics, racism, violence—boil a rage that is the center of much of rap's incendiary lyrics."

But by June of 2002, as the rappers got more explicit about how they turned out their black "hos," *Essence* magazine had a different take to offer its black women readers. Writer Joan Morgan acknowledged in the pages of *Essence* that rap music had become so abusive of women, so full of self-hate for all black people, that it was no longer possible to buy the excuses. She owned up to the fact that five years earlier she would have been writing about the problem of critics trying to censor rap artists, and admitted to "the guilty pleasure of discarding feminist principles for a few hours of booty-shaking hedonistic abandon." But now she wrote, "we [can] no longer get past the sense of degradation most young women feel while watching rap videos." For the first time, Morgan and *Essence* felt free to say that rap videos took advantage of every "erroneous belief about sensuality related to black women." And with so many fathers absent in black homes, the article argued, that "the majority of black girls are ill-equipped to handle this onslaught of sexually degrading content . . . as women we cannot abdicate the responsibility we have to our children. As female hip-hop fans we can no longer afford to buy into the music's most clichéd disclaimer—that rap's content is intended for mature audiences."

The newly bold approach led *Essence* in 2002 to propose that its readers protect their children and themselves with a boycott against rap video shows and the firms that advertise on the shows.

By January of 2005, after the Spelman students forced Nelly to run away for fear of having no explanation—except a willingness to do anything to make a dollar—for his base depictions of black women, the magazine expressed an even deeper militancy to its take on rap. "In [today's] videos are bikini-clad sisters gyrating around . . . like Vegas strippers on meth . . . when we search for ourselves in [the] music . . . we only seem to find our bare breasts and butts . . . the damage of this imbalanced portrayal of black women is impossible to measure. An entire generation of black girls is being raised on these narrow images."

By August of 2005, *Essence* was in a fury over the way rappers gloried in disgracing black women. The recipe for a hit rap record, the magazine announced, was to "throw a few 'bitches' and 'hos' in your lyrics . . . [and refer] to ways to keep a woman in check." As evidence they cited Snoop Dogg's lines: "Can you control your ho? . . . Listen you've got to put that bitch in her place, even if it is slapping her in her face." And they mentioned that Mr. Dogg recently appeared at the MTV Music Awards accompanied by virtually naked girls being pulled along by dog leashes. That led the magazine to come to grips with a reality they had avoided even as they became critical. For the first time they conceded that much of rap had become pornographic. In fact, Snoop, they pointed out correctly, had gone into the porno business along with other rappers such as 50 Cent and Lil Jon. Snoop's *Doggy Style* porn video was the top-selling porn tape of 2001. His video *Snoop Dogg's Hustlaz: Diary of a Pimp* was the top selling X-rated video for 2003.

The bracing reality of black women being pimped to perform sex acts on videos hosted by rappers cut through years of excuses and cheap defenses. So this was the authentic black experience that rappers had been protecting with their rants against censors. They demanded the right to reduce black women to sexually obsessed animals to be put on display like a carnival act in pornography. This was the "keeping it real" bottom line: all black women are sexually crazed, lack discrimination about men, and deserve to be treated as mindless bitches—dogs. This was the flower of the hip-hop art that for years won the protection of black intelligentsia. This was the corruption that had been protected from anyone who dared to say that much rap music had become a vile cesspool, a self-defeating soundtrack to black life that was destroying black pride and purpose in the long history of standing up for equal rights. The rappers silenced responsible black leaders by calling them censors and white-acting prudes who had lost touch with the black community. It was all so they could continue spouting their destructive drivel while community leaders were reduced to shaking their heads.

The consequence of black leaders failing to speak out against the corruption of rap for all those years resulted in real damage to the most vulnerable of black America—poor children, boys and girls, often from broken homes. As a group, they were desperately searching for black pride in the sea of images being thrown at them on TV, on the radio, on the Internet, and in advertising. What those children found was a larger-than-life rapper who was materialistic, sexist, and violent, and used the word *nigger* as a casual description of all black people. It was a musical minstrel show that would have been a familiar delight to nineteenth-century slave owners.

In fact, there are similarities between the economics of slavery and the modern rap industry. Cheap labor, slaves, made it possible for the Southern plantation to make money. All that was required was silent assent to a hellish compromise with the obvious immorality of slavery by the politicians, the religious leaders, the bankers, and the newspaper editors. Cosby is particularly critical of the *New York Times* for a "liberal, patronizing attitude" toward black culture in which they promote hip-hop to show "they are so cool" but fail to write about its negative impact on the black community.

In today's rap business, young musicians hungry for stardom are cheap labor, able to satisfy white America's continuing desire to see Jim Crow jump in blackface minstrel shows. The problem is that the white-owned corporations making big money off the music have to get past the risk of facing charges of promoting racial stereotypes. That requires the silence of black leaders, politicians of all colors, ministers, and the media. Unfortunately for these media giants, which see a profitable market ready for modern minstrel shows, there is the matter of social responsibility. Even in the 1950s, before the *Brown* decision and Dr. King's call to conscience and brotherhood, corporations had trouble getting away with minstrel shows. The TV show *Amos 'n' Andy*, playing on the stereotype of blacks as buffoons, drew so many charges of racism that it had to be taken off the air.

The contemporary answer to this corporate public-relations problem is to have black rappers, in exchange for cash, defend their minstrel show as art and claim their right to freedom of speech. The rappers also argue that their rank depictions of black women and glorifications of violence are simply a reflection of the "authentic" black experience. Oh, so why is it that the biggest consumers of rap music are white men? Why are 80 percent of all hip-hop music customers white?

Statistics show that black men, black women, and white women don't buy even half of the rap music purchased by white men, mostly high-school- and college-age boys. The attraction of the music is its crass, pornographic approach to sex and its crass, racist indulgence in stereotypes of black people. This is an invitation for immature white males to indulge their basest feelings about women and blacks. Advertisers will do anything to penetrate this lusty, beer-drinking demographic even if black women get crushed along the way. White women are not exactly queens in this fantasy world, either. But they can at least join their boyfriends in the pleasure of rebelling against their parents by losing all restraint, sowing their oats with wild partying to rap. And white women have no vested, personal interest in arguing against images of black people as oversexed, overly violent, and overtly stupid. After all, those are black performers in the videos, not white people in blackface. Black people are performing in those videos, not the Ku Klux Klan.

With black musicians as the face of the business, white corporations had the power to portray black people as a debased lot, the "other" in American life, people who are not like hardworking white people; people who don't deserve to be treated as loving family men and women, with ambition, intellect, and faith in God, worthy of trust. Polls of white Americans show that they generally view blacks as less hardworking, less patriotic, and less intelligent than whites. These opinions are generally not voiced openly, but they express themselves in continued bias in hiring, housing, and education. Rap music allows the private sentiment of white males to come into public light with inoculation against any charges of racism. It is a money-maker.

In 2001, rap sold more than country music and became the most popular genre of music in America. In October of 2003, *Billboard* magazine, which tracks the recording industry, had rappers in most of the top ten spots of its list of "Hot 100" acts. And in 2004 a hip-hop act, OutKast, won the nation's top musical award, the Grammy, for Album of the Year. That success is also present in hip-hop fashion, the baggy pants (which mimic the garb of black prisoners, who are forbidden to have belts), the puffy jackets (perfect for hiding guns and packets of drugs), and work boots (that fit the menacing, ex-convict, thug image along with gang tattoos or tattoos in memory of those dead from gang wars and drugs). Hip-hop fashion for women amounts to dressing in the eye-catching clothes of a streetwalker, with added touches of sexually suggestive tattoos just above their butts and pierced navels. The hip-hop look and attitude is reflected as popular culture in movies, TV shows, and commercials. The music long ago became an industry, and all of it is based on silence from black leaders in the face of self-hate, racism, violence, and abuse of women.

Without that silence, white corporate captains, and their hired black faces, could not get away with it.

Black corporate captains have taken their pound of flesh, too.

Robert Johnson's Black Entertainment Television (before it was sold to Viacom) made its money with rap videos that relied heavily on half-naked black women and gangster violence. The use of BET to promote rap meant that all of rap's poisonous images were mainlined directly into the minds of black children. Bill Cosby told this author that the debauchery in BET videos became the strongest influence on black people in their teens and early twenties, replacing the values and the models of success that went missing with absent voices of parents and civil rights leaders.

Young black people watch TV more than do Hispanic or white children. They are searching for a reflection of themselves, an identity in a society that gives them little affirmation. And they are the lion's share of BET's audience. The deluge of guns, half-naked women, and odes to quickie sex, interspersed with advertisements for alcohol, produced a lot of sadness and head-shaking by black leaders, but no outright condemnation. But BET's executives wanted to get closer to the kind of outright pornography that could really bring the ratings up and sell CDs. So BET created a program just for that genre, but broadcast it well after midnight. Their defense of broadcasting *Uncut*, a show full of vile images of black people, was that it was intended for adults only and aired well out of prime time. With tape machines whirring at whatever hour it was broadcast, the show became such a hit that record companies began to make even more explicit versions of their already raunchy videos just for *Uncut*.

To keep the critics quiet so they could make money with this new low of debauchery, BET executives claimed to be meeting audience demand. But those kinds of videos did not appear on their white counterpart, MTV. The only reason BET could get away with such exploitation was that it had black faces in management to offer rationalizations in response to any critic who said the company made money by demeaning black people with the worst possible images of black life. BET followed up that scummy performance with a reality show called *College Hill*. The show was taped at Southern University in Baton Rouge, a mostly black school. The focus was partying, football games, feuds, and sex. The soundtrack was all hip-hop, and so was the identity of the young black women who got air time, the ones who dressed like strippers and knew how to shake that thing. The men got on camera by showing off their "pimped out" cars and bragging about their sexual conquests. Again, young black people nationwide saw the BET stamp of approval on the crippling message that their true black identity was as pimps, whores, and gangsters. And again there was shocking silence from black leaders.

Silence was the response again, as the same cancer spread to video games. The genre is full of hip-hop influence, and is another market where white men again are the dominant consumers. A study by the group Children Now found that nearly 90 percent of the heroes and stars in video games were white men, while 90 percent of black women were "victims of violence," which was twice the rate for white women. Similarly, about 80 percent of black men in the videos were caricatured as verbally loud and physically aggressive, if not crazed with violent behavior. Most the black male characters were musclebound athletes. Fewer than 50 percent of white males fit in the physically aggressive category, but most of the Asians, male and female, were kung-fu-type fighters. These games, marketed to children, capitalize on the big business of allowing people to engage in racial stereotyping. And again there is a high cost for black kids, who are a major consumer market for video games, because the games are based on the fun of engaging in racial stereotyping, including giving permission for white people to stereotype black people as one-dimensional characters focused on their bodies—sexual, violent, and athletic. This is a version of blackness that is a white stereotype.

The corruption of black identity is on display on the streets of black neighborhoods. David Nicholson, a black man, wrote in the *Washington Post* of watching black students on their way to his local high school in D.C. He saw young people carrying few books but doing a lot of cursing, fighting, pot-smoking, and even engaging in public sex acts. "Sometimes, watching students coming and going from Coolidge High School," he said, "I wonder if Americans would have supported the goals of the civil rights movement if they'd known these children would be among its inheritors. . . . Did all those who suffered and died for freedom, all the martyrs of the civil rights movement, such as Medgar Evers, Michael Schwerner, Andrew Goodman, James Chaney, and Martin Luther King Jr., really give their lives so that a generation of young blacks could act out in public as if they were characters in a 'gangsta' movie or rap song?"

Nicholson's lament is echoed by a New York junior high school principal who told *Essence* she sent black girls home repeatedly for "coming to school in the hooker wear they see in these videos." Thomas Rasheed, an associate professor at Florida A&M University, told the magazine *Black Issues in Higher Education* that all too many of his students had "their priorities all wrong," as evidenced by the time they spent getting their hair and nails done to look like women in rap videos. "Some of their skirts are so short you can see their panties," he said. "I have had to tell students not to come to my classes dressed that way." And teachers nationwide complain about the boys in every high school class who spend their mental energy scrawling rap ditties instead of studying because they believe they will be the next big rapper. Meanwhile, they dress like rappers (who dress like black prisoners) and act hard-core, using *nigger*, cursing, and fighting on the way to school, in school, and after school—assuming they are still in school. If they are still there, it is not for education, but because it is their social club.

This is in all in line with Bill Cosby's cutting retort to his critics that their "dirty laundry" is on the street when school gets out at 2:30 p.m. everyday.

Further testimony to the damage done to young black minds by rap comes from Brent Staples, an editorial writer for the *New York Times*. After he heard a 2005 CD from New York City rapper 50 Cent, he wrote that "inner-city listeners who are already at risk of dying prematurely are being fed a toxic diet of rap cuts that glorify murder and make it seem perfectly normal to spend your life in prison."

Added evidence for Staples's point of view came from the CD's title, *The Massacre*. And then there was the cover art. It featured a shotgun aimed at the world, while photographs illustrating the notes inside depicted what Staples described "every ghetto stereotype" from drug dealing to pimping. While this may titillate a mostly white audience, it leaves young black people, especially poor kids searching for identity, with the poisonous idea that middle-class normalcy and achievement are "white" while "authentically black" behavior is tied to violence, illiteracy, and drug dealing. Staples wrote that rap music is now "a medium for worshiping misogyny, materialism, and murder," and it's selling that nihilism to vulnerable young black people who then mimic that behavior on the streets.

Actually, any doubt about the willingness of 50 Cent to make a buck at the cost of twisting young black minds was removed in an earlier CD when he offered his take on male and female relationships. There was no soulful love song, not even a charming or smart seduction. On the contrary, he rapped to women in the dance club that he was not into making love, he just wanted raw sex. Now *there* is a healthy message, ready for repeated broadcast on radio, TV, and dance-hall loudspeakers to a community struggling with high rates of women giving birth outside of marriage.

The lack of positive messages in rap music, its disdain for uplift and inspiration, leads to a question: What is the strategy it proposes for a young soul seeking the good life? The rappers never answer the question directly, so let's listen and look at their art. The answer is obvious at a glance. Black boys can get the good life by becoming rappers or gang members. Angry faces and sullen attitudes are a must. And that will lead them to a life where they can flaunt rolled-up wads of cash, gold chains, diamond-studded watches, and the latest Air Jordan sneakers. Success for young black women is reduced to being boy toys—pure sexual objects, displaying lots of midriff, cleavage, and brightly colored thong panties that are in plain sight above skirts and jeans that slip far below their waist.

"People putting their clothes on backwards, isn't that a sign of something going on wrong?" Cosby asked, describing hip-hop fashion. "Are you not paying attention? People with their hat on backwards, pants down around the crack. Isn't that a sign of something, or are you waiting for Jesus to pull his pants up? Isn't it a sign of something when she's got her dress all the way up to the crack and got all kinds of needles and things going through her body?"

Totally lost to the hip-hop crowd is the idea of this generation of black people having identity far deeper than the latest over-priced T-shirt from a hip-hop clothing company. That deeper identity for this generation of black Americans is a part of the arc of struggle for equal rights, education, and opportunity in America. But the current hip-hop identity does not allow for any hint that doors have opened to black America since the *Brown* decision. The crucial idea that this generation has an unprecedented opportunity to rise up in America and establish itself through education, discipline, and even sacrifice is totally absent. And when it appears, it is dismissed as stupid. Why? The only real black man or woman in rap is a victim whose street credibility comes from being a victim, disrespected, and on the way to jail. That is why the wisdom offered in contemporary rap is a paean to the virtue of being a mindless, vacant soul intent on short-term gratification. What else makes sense for a victim of society? As a critic once wrote in *The Atlantic Monthly*: "Rap is strictly first-person singular." Behind the thumping beat is the message that building a family, a community, and political coalitions are all bad bets. Parents nurturing children and believing in education as a long-term investment is also for suckers.

John McWhorter, a conservative black social critic, views rap's core message as encouraging a young black man to nurture "a sense of himself as an embattled alien in his own land. It is difficult to see how this can lead to anything but dissension and anomie." On the other hand, it is easy to see how rap leads young black people to dismiss political activism and dismiss building coalitions across racial lines to create social change. It is also easy to see how rap is leading young people to take on the identity of doomed victims. In the world of rap, only suckers believe that America is a land of opportunity, even though that very idea continues to attract millions to the United States from around the world.

This defeatism is not a secret to anyone who follows the rap industry. The refrain is that "keepin' it real" means believing that you have no future, that you revel in materialistic excess, and take advantage of other black people (kill the men and treat the women like animals). Nick Crowe, in an essay in *Prospect* magazine in 2004, wrote that rap has "endless appetite for self-gratification, its self-destructive nature [contributing] nothing to the community." Crowe added that rap celebrated feuds between its stars, which led to the deaths of rival rappers Tupac Shakur and Notorious BIG, who inspired young black men to join the gangster life, to live large for the moment with guns and fast money. The result, he concluded, is that rap's message is one of cruel "disempowerment rather than opportunity." And while the "keepin' it real" pledge might appear to be a call for black solidarity, he noted, "scratch a little deeper and the words 'Don't Change' emerge. . . . 'Keepin' it real' hinders change, both social and musical."

But that leads to a question. If rap is so crippling to young black people, why is the same music with the same lyrics nothing more than a diversion to young white people, a majority of its patrons? Defenders of the most violent and sexist rap also point out that the rap industry is so profitable and culturally dominant that whites are trying to get into the game, for example, the successful Vanilla Ice and the even more successful Eminem. As for the sex side of the business, rap's die-hard defenders say white girls like Paris Hilton and the babes in the popular "Girls Gone Wild" videos are doing the same thing that black girls are doing in rap videos.

The flaw in this argument is that young black people and young white people are not equal in America. Paris Hilton, for one, is an heiress. If she appears in a sex video and behaves like a goof, it actually gets her publicity and advances her career. Even the white girls in "Girls Gone Wild" appear to be on spring break from college. Many are on their way to getting a college degree. Some young black women fit the same model, but the Census Bureau tells us that when it comes to high school and college graduation rates, most young black women are still trailing most young white women. More black women live in poverty. They have more children out of wedlock. And black women are more likely to end up on welfare.

To cut to the heart of the monster, poor black women are being asked to dance along to lies that are undercutting their chances for success. They are huge consumers of popular culture, especially music and television. They are the disadvantaged black girls who attend bad big-city schools and struggle to identify an older male who believes in their intellect and character. Those young women are trying to find a way to feel good about their identity in a culture that gives little reinforcement to black women. Rap's pumped-up message to them is to get naked and shake it before giving it up to do the wild thing. They are literally described in this music as whores, sluts, bobbing chicken heads, and of course bitches. As a success strategy for young black women, that is a disaster, and yet the rappers and the corporations behind them have been given a free pass to sell this poison for years.

Louis Farrakhan, head of the Nation of Islam, gave a speech about this point in 2001 at a New York hip-hop summit. He warned the rappers that they were "being used by the enemy so that [black people] will destroy each other." Rappers glamorize guns, he said, but he said the hip-hop industry was a worldwide phenomenon because of the power of words, not guns. Farrakhan, his face full of anguish, told the rappers they have "become tools of a satanic mind that will use you to destroy" black people. People might be dancing to their music, he said, and excited about the glamour of their hip-hop videos that glorify a lifestyle of jewelry, sex, cognac, and big cars, but the negative impact of rap's content, he argued, is eating away at the roots of black life. "When you are a rapper and you understand your leadership role, you must understand that with leadership comes responsibility. You did not ask for it . . . but you now have to accept responsibility . . . What do you have to say about the abuse of women, the pedophiles that are going around? You are the teacher. Can you teach that where there are no decent women, there are no decent men, for the woman is the mother of civilization? Can you teach young people to admire women and not abuse women, to respect and honor women and not defile women? Can you teach like that?"

Cosby recounted to this author a conversation among teenaged boys he visited in a classroom. The boys told him they did not expect to live beyond the age of twenty-eight—some of them said twenty-five. "If you don't expect to be alive beyond twenty-five, it is easy to do certain things, like make a lot of babies without worrying about taking care of them," said Cosby. "You don't care if you give AIDS to a woman. And the women don't care if they have baby after baby, because they don't believe they are going to raise those babies." And there is no shame, he added. When he grew up in Philadelphia, Cosby said, a man who got a woman pregnant without marrying her often left town or went in the military or to a reform school. Now it is acceptable behavior, celebrated in hip-hop's corrosive culture.

And it has an effect on the way whites see blacks, too. The rappers then reinforce in the minds of those wild white frat boys—later to become our corporate captains and managers—that black women are sexually indiscriminate, stupid, greedy, and lazy. Young black men are thugs, and, in the words of music critic Stanley Crouch, "monkey-moving, gold-chain-wearing, illiteracy-spouting, penis-pulling, sullen, combative buffoons." Who would hire such a person? Who would want to live next to them? Who would want to help them? Yet this message is sent worldwide by the $4-billion industry in rap music, fashion, and advertising. This is a twenty-first-century version of D. W. Griffith's *Birth of a Nation*, the 1915 film that demonized former slaves as rapists, murders, and thieves while glorifying the KKK.

But that is not enough. It was up to Snoop Dogg to take it to new lows with his pornographic videos. He played the clown as a black man. He spoke some indecipherable pidgin English that allowed white people to laugh at his ignorance. Next, he came out as a pure pimp. Snoop's game has gone so low that there is no defense remaining. He has made it clear that rap has become America's late-night masturbatory fantasy.

He wants to be the ringmaster. Racial stereotypes, violence, and abuse of women are all in the house, dragged in the door for a make-believe private party, a carnival of people dressed in hip-hop fashion, sipping the obligatory expensive champagne and cognac, while gangster drug dealers and their thugs offer the edgy fear of gunplay. In the center ring, porn-star women break-dance.

Millionaire black athletes, preferably basketball players, and Asian kung-fu fighters circulate at the party to fill out the·stereotypes. Young white men are clamoring to get in and be cool, too. Young black people want to an invite to the party, too. Any concern about racism, criminality, and abuse of women is put to rest by black rappers, like Snoop, in service to white corporations. They assure us all that this excess is the real black experience. The counterculture that fueled black music and protest music has been reduced to a marketing strategy for sneakers and cell-phone ring tones.

A long time ago, one of the early rap groups, Public Enemy, rapped about the need to "Fight the Power." The energy in that music was its willingness to confront establishment and stereotypes. Rap is now the exact opposite. It is not progressive, but an essential part of a greedy corporate culture that needs cover for using racist stereotypes, violence, and misogyny to make its products cool and attract people with disposable income, mostly the young white male market. Generations of black music found a way to tell our story, full of joy, pain, and defiance—making a way out of no way. The music had so much soul it was called "soul music." Too much hip-hop has become soulless music. It revels in the pathology of black life, degrades our women, and reduces our men to murderers. With the help of corporate backers, hip-hop does its damage to vulnerable black minds, plants negative attitudes about black people in white American minds, and also sends the message around the world, damaging the image of black people in a global economy.

Dr. William C. Banfield, head of the American Cultural Studies program at the University of St. Thomas, once said of rappers: "They are the biggest black sellouts of all time because they allow the white media structure to lessen the potential of a balanced picture of black people in contemporary American cultural projection." And Harry Belafonte, the singer, said much the same when he described rappers as "caught in a trick bag because it's a way to make unconscionable sums of money and a way to absent yourself from any sense of moral responsibility." Spike Lee, the movie director, made much the same point in a film about black advertising executives making money by selling depraved images of black people. The movie was aptly called *Bamboozled*, as in confused and lost, used and abused while you think you are using the other guy.

Unquestionably, money is to be made by pandering to the worst instincts in the human soul and driving popular culture into the dirt. Comedy Central, the cable channel, was willing to give Dave Chappelle, the black comic, a $50-million contract to put on a minstrel show complete with pimps, whores, and Rick James yelling "bitch." At one taping in 2004, Chappelle was doing a skit in blackface about a magical black pixie that tries to convince black people to play out the worst stereotypes, when a white man on the set laughed out loud, and Chappelle stopped the taping. He found the man's reaction so shocking that, as he told *Time* magazine, "My head almost exploded." He said he began to think he was no longer satirizing racial stereotypes but reinforcing them. That is the sad reality of hip-hop and much of Chappelle's comedy. Eventually he walked away from the $50-million deal for no official reason. Maybe his conscience couldn't take it anymore.

Bill Cosby finds the critics and fans who praise Chappelle "deeply confused," he said in interview for this book. He called Chappelle's act the "modern Stepin Fetchit," a minstrel show intended to diminish black people. He is outraged that a Harvard law professor, Randall Kennedy, wrote a book titled *Nigger*, so that people can "walk around and use that word, including people who don't like you." Cosby remembers watching a tribute to Richard Pryor after Pryor, a ribald comedian, won the coveted

Mark Twain Award. Pryor, who often used the word in his routines, came back from a trip to Africa and announced he would never use that word again because of a personal epiphany in which he discovered there are "no niggers in Africa." But at the nationally televised tribute to Pryor, *nigger* was used by one young black comic after another. "A friend called me in a low voice to say how embarrassing it was to see those people up there felt so free to use that word," Cosby said. His critique extends to sports. He is a fan of the basketball player Allen Iverson, but he is furious that the 76ers star wants to "rap about thugs" instead of the "desire and discipline it takes to be a successful athlete."

When Cosby asks black people to take a measure of their progress fifty years after the *Brown* decision, he is calling out parents and their children who delight in ignorance and ignorant, shame-faced comedy. He is calling out people who brag about a disregard for school and deny their role in a continuing civil rights struggle that requires discipline, sacrifice, and responsibility for one's brother. Cosby's critics shot back that he was ignoring the "systemic racism" in American education, employment, and housing that holds back poor black people. Where are Cosby's critics when young black people are so brainwashed by the system they can't see that they are being manipulated by ad agencies to buy overpriced clothes, sunglasses, and hubcaps so they can become fashion gurus for white suburban kids? Where are Cosby's critics when poor black kids are tricked into celebrating intentional ignorance as "keepin' it real"? Where is the critical revulsion at greed from the likes of BET in electronically pimping black women as sluts and bitches?

The silence is louder than the thumping bass line of the hip-hop beat. It is so loud it hurts ears, hearts, and souls. It is a total beatdown on black people.

7

FORGOTTEN HISTORY

WITH ALL THE CONTROVERSY, it is easy to forget the words of thanks and praise in Bill Cosby's speech celebrating the fiftieth anniversary of the *Brown* decision. He called out the names of civil rights activists who worked on the *Brown* case: NAACP lawyers; the psychologist Kenneth Clark; the head of the National Council of Negro Women, Dorothy Height. Cosby praised young black people of that era who "marched and were hit in the face with rocks," especially the Little Rock Nine, who faced angry mobs to get into a high school that remained segregated even after *Brown* was the law.

The media coverage of Cosby's speech overlooked his celebration of those civil rights heroes. It is not news when a celebrity says nice things about a civil rights group. That is expected at a benefit dinner or a gala commemoration. But what the reporters missed was that Cosby's praise was not limited to past victories by very old people. Cosby praised their dreams, their expectation of what future generations of black people could do in an America with less outright segregation. The idea of a better future for black people, growing from the work done by civil rights heroes fifty years ago, is at the heart of the power of Cosby's speech, because he played old heroes and modern villains against each other.

"I have to apologize to [Dr. Kenneth Clark] for these people [today] because Kenneth said it straight," Cosby told the Constitution Hall crowd. "He said you [black people] have to strengthen yourselves . . . and everybody said it. Julian Bond said it. Dick Gregory said it. All these lawyers said it. And [now, fifty years later] you wouldn't know that anybody had done a damned thing."

Dr. Clark performed the famous "Dolls Test," a psychological study of black children in South Carolina that found segregated schools made them feel inferior to white children—less intelligent, less attractive, and less capable. Thurgood Marshall, the top lawyer at the NAACP Legal Defense and Education Fund, included Clark's research in the brief he sent to the Supreme Court in advance of oral arguments in the *Brown* case. Fifty years later, Clark did not make it to Washington for the celebration because of health problems (that led to his death in May 2005). But his spirit was front and center because Cosby spoke repeatedly about him.

"Kenneth Clark, somewhere in his home in upstate New York. . . . Thank God he doesn't know what's going on. Thank God," said Cosby.

God was another central player in Cosby's speech. By Cosby's account, Jesus Christ, the Holy Spirit, and God Almighty himself helped the civil rights workers who defeated legal segregation. The activists faced politically powerful, rich segregationists who controlled most of the nation's policemen and judges. The Holy Trinity also had to hold back deeply held white male fears of what might happen in school if black boys sat next to white girls. And God had to have a hand in making presidents and senators do the right thing by passing laws (the 1964 Civil Rights Act and the 1965 Voting Rights Act) despite their fear of losing votes from segregationists. Who else but God could speak to white hearts about ending the widespread white acceptance in the 1950s of the idea that blacks were an inferior race who deserved second-class citizenship?

After all that God had done to make *Brown* a victory for people seeking racial justice over the last fifty years, Cosby said, it is now time for black people to stop asking God for help.

"You can't keep asking that God will find a way," he said. "God is tired of you. God was there when they won all those cases . . . that is where God was because these people were doing something. And God said, 'I'm going to find a way.' I wasn't there when God said it—I'm making this up. But it sounds like what God would do." And now, Cosby added, speaking of the heroes who struggled and sacrificed to win the *Brown* case with God's help, "They've got to be wondering what the hell happened."

Of course, America's struggle to achieve liberty and justice for all goes beyond *Brown*. Centuries of struggle set the stage for the *Brown* decision. Black people have been advocating for equal opportunity in America as far back as the 1600s. Beginning with slavery and denial of full citizenship rights—slaves being considered three-fifths of a man in the original constitution—there has been an epic, centuries-long confrontation with racism led by African Americans. The vision of the prize for this movement was liberation. Freeing black people from slavery was the first goal. That resulted in the Emancipation Proclamation. The next step in the struggle was to establish individual rights protected without regard to race. Black people wanted equal rights to profit from their work, to be protected from racial violence, to educate their children, to own land and run businesses, as well as to vote and be given respect on an equal basis with other citizens. The expectation was always that black success was inevitable once black people controlled their future. In that picture, the only limits on future black success came from racists.

And that is why Cosby felt the need to apologize to Kenneth Clark and to God. A generation dropping out of school and celebrating the gangster life is a shocking turn of events, a repudiation of hundreds of years of the civil rights struggle. It is a rejection of the gift of opportunity. It is collective act of contempt for the true black American identity—a strong, creative, loving people with deep faith in God, seeking a better life for the next generation.

When Cosby complains about the sight of young black people loitering outside of school, cursing, fighting, and getting high, he paints a picture of twenty-first-century black people who are turning their backs on their own history. That image is the opposite of young black people who wanted a good education so much that they faced the danger of walking through segregationist mobs intent on keeping them out of previously all-white schools. That history is miles away from any person of color turning his or her back on education and giving in to a popular culture that makes black people out to be nothing but gangsters, using *nigger* and destroying the English language.

That history is compelling.

There is no better example of this powerful legacy than what happened in Little Rock, Arkansas, in 1957. Three years after the *Brown* decision, almost all Southern school districts engaged in a "massive resistance" campaign against school integration. In fact, most school districts in all areas of the country kept black children in shoddy schools, with third-rate books and supplies. The Supreme Court opened the door to this defiance a year after the *Brown* decision. In 1955 the high court ruled that school districts could be "deliberate," or take their time about breaking down school segregation. That opened the door to stalling by politicians, who used the time to whip up opposition to any racial mixing at school.

Georgia's governor, Herman Talmadge, advised whites in his state to dismiss the *Brown* decision as a "mere scrap of paper." He gave fiery speeches about the "chaos" that was sure to come from bringing students of all races together in one school. He stirred sexual fears when he said black children and white children going to school together would lead to intermarriage and result in "mongrelization of the races." In Arkansas, Governor Orval Faubus announced that he had conducted a poll that found 85 percent of his state's residents opposed school integration. Portraying the people of Arkansas and the entire South as victims of powerful federal authorities, he pledged not to let the federal court run over the will of the state. It was an appeal that revived anger over the Civil War and the Confederate rallying cry of "states' rights," which would allow them to continue slavery without having to obey the federal government. That anger was still boiling below the surface nearly a hundred years later, and now segregationists, furious over the *Brown* decision, called on that memory to mount opposition to school integration.

Black parents and children became the targets for this anger. In Virginia's Prince Edward County the segregationists closed all public schools to prevent integration. Private academies for white children opened to avoid orders for racial integration. The black children were left with no schools at all. Even where the public schools remained open, black students faced high hurdles to get into the more-modern, better-funded schools operated for white children. In Little Rock, Arkansas, the school superintendent put in place a plan to begin integrating just two high schools. But even that was too much for the school board. They voted to limit integration to one high school, Central High, three years after *Brown*. All the other schools in the city would be integrated over the next six years.

By dumping the superintendent's plan, the school board angered NAACP lawyers, who filed suit against the delay. But a federal court of appeals ruled that the school board's slow, small plan met with the Supreme Court's call for school integration with "all deliberate speed." And to punish the NAACP for filing that suit, the state legislature passed laws making it optional for white children to attend integrated schools.

In Little Rock the school board decided they now had the upper hand, and announced a reduction in the number of black students to be allowed into Central High School. They even threatened to sue black families who had been involved in the losing NAACP suit unless their children agreed not to go to Central. Initially, seventy-five black students had signed up to transfer to Central High, but after the school board started scaring them off, only twenty-five students kept their names on the list. That was still too much for the segregationists. School officials made threatening phone calls to black students who played sports or studied music. They warned that black athletes and performers might be kept off any of Central's school teams and the orchestra, and denied roles in school plays. Most of the black parents decided they did not want to put their children through that kind of humiliation, and pulled their children out of plans to attend Central High. Only nine black students and their parents remained committed to showing up for the first day of school.

That was still too many black people for Governor Faubus. He went on television to tell the entire state that he was placing the national guard around Central High to keep out the "Little Rock Nine." The school board advised black parents not to take their children to school because the sight of black adults and the national guard might incite white mob violence. With the possibility of armed military action, the nine black students stayed away on the first day of school. The school superintendent promised to protect the black students if they showed up the next day. But when one black girl, Elizabeth Eckford, arrived by herself that morning, the national guard raised bayonets to block her from going into the school. And a group of jeering whites began shouting, "Lynch her!" She was understandably traumatized and had to be escorted away. The other eight black students did not get into the school that day, either.

It was not until more than two weeks later that students got a police escort to get them into Central High through a side door. As news spread about their presence inside the school, a mob gathered outside. By lunchtime the black students had to be taken out of school by the police and driven thorough the crowd. The mayor of Little Rock then sent an emergency wire asking President Eisenhower to send federal troops to protect the black students. Only because of that federal protection did students finally make their way into the front door of the school. They were kicked and cursed and generally harassed on a daily basis.

In May, one student did graduate. Ernest Green became the first black person to get a Central High diploma. And when he crossed the stage there was no applause—just silence from the white audience. The next school year, all of Little Rock's schools were closed, and half of the white students enrolled in private segregationist academies. The city's black students had no schools to attend. The U.S. Supreme Court had to review the situation and ordered that the schools be reopened and integrated. That didn't happen until 1959.

The history in Little Rock is a sharp contrast to Bill Cosby's stories about the high percentage of young black people dropping

out of school, embracing the "thug life," and wasting the opportunities that the *Brown* decision opened for them.

And Little Rock is not a one-time event in black history. Sacrifices had to be made time and time again to keep the movement
moving forward. At the University of Mississippi in 1962, James
Meredith's insistence on entering that school led to segregationist
resistance and gunfire that killed two. Twenty-eight U.S. marshals were shot.

The governor, Ross Barnett, had promised segregationists in
his state that no black person would attend "Ole Miss." He went
on statewide television to say the idea of a black man sitting in
classes at the University of Mississippi was a threat to white civilization and "our greatest crisis since the War Between the States."
Appealing to white fear, Governor Barnett added, "There is no
case in history where the Caucasian race has survived social integration." Just days before the segregationist riot at the university
to stop Meredith from registering, the governor told a crowd at
the Saturday college football game (many of them waving Confederate flags), that "I love Mississippi, I love her people, her cus-
toms. . . . Never shall our emblem go from Colonel Reb to Old
Black Joe." And once the violence ended and he had registered,
Meredith had to be guarded on campus by federal marshals.

One of Meredith's key supporters was Medgar Evers, Mississippi field secretary for the NAACP. Evers was killed less than a
year later, in the summer of 1963, by a sniper as he took the drive
to end segregation beyond the university and to the city of Jackson, the state capital. In a speech just a month before his assassination, describing life in Jackson for black people, Evers said
black people were "refused admittance to the city auditorium and
the coliseum; his children refused a ticket to a good movie in a
downtown theater; his wife and children refused service at a lunch

counter in a downtown store where they trade. . . . He sees a city of 150,000, of which forty percent is Negro, in which there is not a single Negro policeman or policewoman, school crossing guard, fireman, clerk, stenographer. . . . He sees local hospitals which segregate Negro patients."

A sit-in by the NAACP at a segregated Woolworth's lunch counter in downtown Jackson ended up with white thugs attacking demonstrators by throwing pepper in their eyes and dumping paint on them. When black students sang songs about freedom and civil rights during their lunch hour at a segregated black school, the police appeared with attack dogs and then began beating the students while the dogs bit them and ripped their clothes. Evers refused to back down. After a concert by famed singer Lena Horne raised money to get demonstrators out of jail, Evers told the crowd they had to do more than give money. He wanted them to get involved in the demonstrations and marches. "Freedom has never been free. . . . I love my children and I love my wife with all my heart," he said. "And I would die, and die gladly, if that would make a better life for them."

Just five days later, Evers was dead from gunshots that hit him as he got out of his car. The man charged with the crime, Byron de la Beckwith, was a member of the all-white Citizens' Council. The gun used to commit the murder belonged to Beckwith, and his fingerprints appeared on the gun's sight, which was found in a separate place. Cab drivers testified that he had asked for directions to Evers's home that night. But two trials ended in a hung jury, and eventually Beckwith ran for lieutenant governor. In 1994, after he had lived free for more than thirty years, a Mississippi jury finally found him guilty of murdering Evers.

Evers's death did not end the movement in Mississippi. The NAACP, the Student Nonviolent Coordinating Committee, the

Congress of Racial Equality, and the Southern Christian Leadership Conference all picked up the effort to get the right to vote for Mississippi's black population. It led to a 1963 effort called "Freedom Vote," in which white students from some of the nation's most prestigious colleges joined with young black southerners to register poor, rural black people to vote. As a follow-up to that effort, the civil rights groups invited more young people to Mississippi for the summer of 1964 to open Freedom Schools to teach young people how to read, write, and do math.

Ten years after *Brown*, there was no school integration in Mississippi, and the black schools were so bad that most black parents in Mississippi did not even bother to send their children to them.

The "Freedom Summer" campaign in 1964 also opened health centers and law offices, in the face of constant threats from all-white local officials who realized that their complete power over poor, uneducated black people was being threatened by the presence of what they called "Northern agitators," the Freedom workers. They complained that Mississippi was being subjected to an "invasion," and the state legislature made it illegal to open a school without a state permit and to hand out leaflets calling for boycotts.

In late June of 1964, one day after the first of the Freedom Summer activists arrived in Mississippi, three of them disappeared. James Chaney, twenty-one, a black student and a native of Mississippi, had been driving two other volunteers to look into why a black church had been burned down in the small town of Lawndale. Along the way, the police in Philadelphia, Mississippi, stopped the car for allegedly speeding. Andrew Goodman, twenty-two, a student from Queens College in New York City, and Michael Schwerner, twenty-four, who lived in Brooklyn, New

York, were also arrested. The two white men and Chaney were handcuffed and taken to jail. The police said they were released that night, but the three civil rights workers were never seen alive again. President Johnson sent two hundred navy men to drag swamps and walk the farmland in search of the men. On August 4, more than a month later, their bodies were found buried in a clay dam on a rural farm. All three had been shot with .38-caliber bullets, and Chaney, the one black activist, had been beaten so badly his skull had been fractured.

At the funeral service for Chaney, David Dennis, the head of CORE in Mississippi, spoke: "We've got to stand up. . . . Don't just look at me and go back and tell folks you've been to a nice service. Your work is just beginning. . . . Stand up! Those neighbors who were too afraid to come to this service, pick them up and take them down there to register to vote. Go down there and do it. Don't ask that white man if you can register to vote. Just tell him: "Baby, I'm here." Stand up. Hold your heads up. Don't bow down anymore. We want our freedom now."

That was the history Bill Cosby talked about when he referred to sacrifices made to open doors to black Americans. It was why he stopped in the middle of his speech at the *Brown* anniversary celebration to apologize to Kenneth Clark and people who "fought so hard," as he put it, and now must be "wondering what the hell happened." It is why the idea of turning away from this passionate, blood-soaked history to drop out of school, to excuse criminals, and to celebrate use of *nigger* is so shocking to Cosby. And Cosby speaks for millions of people, including millions of black people, who can't understand how this inspiring American history can be ignored when it is not being twisted to justify the outrageous libel that black people are weaklings who are owed reparations by the government.

When Rosa Parks died in 2005, fifty years after she started the legendary year-long bus boycott in Montgomery, Alabama, by refusing to give up her seat on a bus, she was honored by having her casket placed in the U.S. Capitol for viewing. People waited in line for hours to walk by the woman who was respectfully known as "the mother of the movement." The strength of a simple woman to defy the power of segregation launched a nonviolent protest in 1955 that created a model for the mass protests. The marches and boycotts that followed led to passage of the 1964 Civil Rights Act and the 1965 Voting Rights Act. Yet the reality of Mrs. Parks's final years included having her house in Detroit broken into by a young black man who robbed her of fifty-four dollars. The sad treatment of Mrs. Parks included the movie *Barbershop*, in which a character says that she did nothing more than sit on her bottom. And when she was in her final years, she had to put up with the unsettling reality of a rap group using her name without her permission to sell their music.

Cosby should have included her when he apologized to Kenneth Clark and others who made sacrifices to open doors only, in the case of Rosa Parks, to end up being robbed and mugged by a young black man. To Rosa Parks it had to be more than sad to see so many people in this generation turn away from black tradition, and reject their turn to be part of a great movement to advance black people in America. During the bus boycott, a reporter asked one elderly black woman why she was not riding the bus, but walking and waiting in long lines to pay for cabs. "I'm doing it for my children and my grandchildren," she said. Now the question, as Cosby sees it, is whether her children and grandchildren understand what that old woman was fighting to achieve.

In her time, Rosa Parks worked with much less opportunity to make a difference for her family or for black people than most black Americans have today. Yet she somehow found a way. The inspiring story of Rosa Parks is that of a woman who had to drop out of segregated schools in rural Alabama because her family had no one else to care for an ailing relative. But she did not quit. After the relative's death, she went back to school, while working another job, and got her high school diploma at age twenty-one. And throughout her life she worked in the local NAACP and with a group of women in Montgomery to take on segregation on the bus lines. She even attended the Highlander Folk School, which trained Southern working-class people, black and white, to build political power by organizing unions, political campaigns, and even teaching the ill-educated how to read and write. The school saw potential in educating poor people, especially poor black people. The poor could be given power by being given the ability to speak up for themselves. All of that work preceded her one moment of refusing to give up her seat to a white man on the bus.

After the Montgomery bus boycott ended successfully, Martin Luther King Jr. wrote that it was a "stride toward freedom" in a book with the same title. At the end of that book, King tried to answer the question of where do people who care about racial justice go beyond the bus boycott. In 1958, King wrote that integration is "not some lavish dish that the federal government or the white liberal will pass out on a silver platter while the Negro merely furnishes the appetite." It sounds as if he was offering an early critique of the drive for reparations.

The real wealth inherited by black people, King said, was being empowered to create positive social change. The success of a bus boycott led by black people—smart, disciplined black people—was a model of new possibilities. King went so far as to say that the triumph changed the self-image of black people. Gone was the shuffling, defeated spirit, and in its place came black people in Montgomery walking tall. King also pointed to the bravery of the Little Rock Nine at Central High School as more newfound wealth for black people, because violence and suffering did not stop determined black people, and now that example was available to inspire a younger generation of Americans, black and white, to act with courage and dignity in the face of suffering.

King, sounding a lot like Bill Cosby fifty years later, then spoke in strong terms about the need for black people to admit when they fell short. He began by saying that black crime rates were too high, that too much drinking and spending on luxury items was wasting black potential for creating positive social change. He even criticized sloppiness and lack of cleanliness: "Even the most poverty-stricken among us can purchase a ten-cent bar of soap. Even the most uneducated among us can have high morals."

Looking around black America, the future Nobel Peace Prize winner said that in every freedom movement some people "prefer to remain oppressed." Even when Moses led the Israelites out of slavery in Egypt, he found that some slaves had "become accustomed to being slaves." King said some slaves preferred "the 'flesh-pots of Egypt' to the ordeals of emancipation." He cautioned black people not to give in to lies, malice, hate, self-indulgence, and self-destruction. King appears to have been setting the agenda for Cosby when he wrote that young black people in his day needed to "improve their general level of behavior," and "Negro parents must be urged to give their children the love, attention, and sense of belonging that a segregated society deprives them of."

King had direct experience with young people as activists. The college students and young activists in groups such as the Student Nonviolent Coordinating Committee had a love-hate relationship with King because he was so popular and respected, and he dominated the media spotlight. But black children had no reservations about the famous minister. He was their hero. They viewed King as a messiah. And King viewed black children as people with a legitimate role in fighting for civil rights.

In 1963 King led demonstrations against segregation in downtown stores in Birmingham. The city was well known to civil rights activists as the site of the bloody 1961 attack by segregationists on young white and black people riding buses together as Freedom Riders to challenge local laws on racial separation. By 1963 Birmingham had a national reputation as "Bombingham," for eighteen bombings of the homes of black activists in five years. The police commissioner, Eugene "Bull" Connor, used his forces to close down any meeting of black activists, and he didn't even have to bother with NAACP meetings because that group had been banned by the state legislature since 1956. That was the same year that a gang of white men dragged the famous black singer Nat "King" Cole off a stage and beat him because they said he was singing love songs to white women. When federal judges ordered swimming pools and parks opened to black people in the late fifties, the white leaders of Birmingham just shut them down.

King's demonstrations infuriated the white leadership of Birmingham, especially the police commissioner, whose men beat the marchers with nightsticks and attacked them with dogs and firehoses. When that didn't stop King from getting more people to march, the police argued that public safety was in jeopardy and got a court injunction against any more marches. But King insisted on marching and was immediately jailed. The jails overflowed with demonstrators by the time of King's arrest, and they were being mistreated as they waited for court hearings. The entire effort seemed on the verge of failure when one of King's aides suggested that it was time to get the city's black schoolchildren to join the marches.

The idea was to make a disturbing display of police arresting children. King agreed, and after difficult conversations with parents who worried about what the police might do to the children, King arranged for the children to come to churches to learn about earlier civil rights marches and protests in other cities. Then King gave a speech to a group of the schoolchildren, aged six to eighteen, telling them that it was their time to get involved in a nonviolent, disciplined show of their power to fight for their future. On the first day, more than nine hundred black children were arrested for protesting segregation. On the next day, more than a thousand children joined the protests and faced Bull Connor's dogs and firehoses. TV cameras recorded the awful sight of black children being knocked off their feet by water shot from firehoses even as they tried to make a determined stand. In some cases, little girls could be seen being rolled down the street by the powerful cascades of water and chased by vicious dogs. The news reports stirred the conscience of the nation. The federal government, including the president, felt pressure to intervene. President John F. Kennedy sent federal troops to Alabama with orders to stand by in defense of the children. With that threat over their heads, the city's businessmen suddenly agreed to a deal to end segregation at lunch counters and department stores, leaving Bull Connor isolated and defeated.

The willingness of black children, under King's direction, to put themselves at risk, to endure suffering, and to go to jail, gave new inspiration to the civil rights movement. It also offered another example of black people taking positive action to help themselves. King's view of the children and their power was evident in a letter he wrote while in jail for demonstrating in Birmingham against court orders. The strategy of using black children as marchers had not yet been put into action when a group of white ministers wrote in a letter to the local newspaper criticizing King for being impatient and creating a dangerous situation in a community struggling with racial issues. From his jail cell, King began writing a response to the ministers in the margins of a newspaper. It was all the paper he had to write on. And the heart of this thoughts concerned black children.

"For years now, I have heard the word 'Wait!'" he wrote.

Perhaps it is easy for those who have never felt the sting-ing darts of segregation to say "Wait." But when you have seen vicious mobs lynch your mothers and fathers . . . when you see the vast majority of your 20 million Negro brothers and sisters in an airtight cage of poverty in the midst of an affluent society; when you suddenly find your tongue twisted and your speech stammering as you seek to explain to your six-year-old daughter why she can't go to the amusement park that has just been advertised on tele-vision and see tears well up in her eyes when she is told that "Funtown" is closed to colored children and see omi-nous clouds of inferiority begin to form in her little men-tal sky, and see her beginning to distort her personality by developing an unconscious bitterness toward white people; when you have to concoct an answer for a five-year-old son who is asking: "Daddy, why do white people treat col-ored people so mean" . . . when you are forever fighting a degenerating sense of "Nobody-ness,"—then you will un-derstand why we find it so difficult to wait.

Toward the end of this passionate "Letter from a Birmingham Jail," King wrote that young people, high school and college stu-dents, were willing to demonstrate and face violent police and be put in jail for the sake of their own conscience. "One day the South will know that when these disinherited children of God sat down at lunch counters, they were in reality standing up for what is best in the American dream and for the most sacred values in our Judeo-Christian heritage."

King's concern with young people was principally that they gain a sense of their power, their spirit, and their ability to insist on equality for themselves. He did not want them to see themselves as victims, as the "other" in American life. If he lived today, King would be appalled at the idea of young black people seeing themselves as nothing but comedians, ballplayers, or gangster rappers. How could he not be furious at young people who lack an appreciation of the historic sacrifices made by young people to open doors for today's young Americans, black, Hispanic, Asian, Native American, and white?

This is the same voice that Bill Cosby used when he spoke with disappointment about twenty-first-century young black people dropping out, hanging out, and walking out on the tradition of dignified black people making sacrifices to advance the common cause of civil rights. Cosby was derided as "out of touch," and for blaming the poor for their troubles. It would have been harder to attack King. But even Dr. King, who in May 2004 would have been seventy-five, would have been dismissed as a cranky old man by the people who jumped on Cosby.

The point, however, is not that we can predict what King's response would have been to Cosby's remarks. The point is that both Cosby and King were saying that young black people should be held to high expectations. The point is that they believed that if young people were seen as capable of leadership, those young people would lead. This is complete respect, even honor, for all young people, but especially for black youth. It is the critics who want to take away their power by telling them they are helpless and capable of nothing more than being cogs in a materialistic media machine that has young people consumed with overpriced clothing, bling-bling, sex, and absurd posturing that fulfills racist stereotypes of black people as violent gangsters.

The adults who led the civil rights movement fifty years ago saw the potential in young black people to reach the "mountain-top." They believed in the idea of struggle and handing a better chance to the next generation. That is why Bill Cosby felt the need to apologize to the Kenneth Clarks, the Little Rock Nine, and even God—all who put themselves on the line during the civil rights revolution of the 1950s and 1960s.

8

LIKE A HURRICANE

WHEN HURRICANE KATRINA HIT the Gulf Coast in late summer 2005, it tore away New Orleans's slick reputation as a steamy, sexy town for conventions, jazz, and good food. The storm exposed a gritty, less attractive reality. The world watched as the levees around New Orleans broke, trapping poor, mostly black people. Chaos and fear rose higher than the dirty waters as poor black people began rushing to dry ground and shelter at the Convention Center and the New Orleans Superdome. They looked like third-world refugees fleeing disaster. But these tragic souls were born in the United States. Their desperation leaped from TV screens around the world as a bitter reminder that despite American affluence, despite the gains of the civil rights movement, and despite the incredible rise of the black middle class, there were lots of poor black people living the American Nightmare that existed alongside the American Dream.

The reality of poor black Americans literally trying to keep their heads above water prompted soul-searching questions about why black Americans are always left behind. Asian immigrants are loading themselves into hulls of cargo ships, risking a suffocating death, to come to America. Mexican immigrants risk death to cross desert sands and avoid border guards so that they can get into the United States. Immigrants from Cuba and Haiti will set out across the ocean in rafts made of inner tubes as they try to make it to America. The bright, luminous attraction of American education, economic opportunity, and political freedom is so magnetic that people from all corners of the globe risk everything to get to the United States.

Here is how Bill Cosby once put it to a group of black high school students in Compton, California: "People from Ethiopia, from Nigeria, who came from a piece of land with a goat want to come to America. We're already here."

To another group in Houston, Cosby said, "I'm going to tell you that the Ethiopian knows the value of an American education. The Nigerian knows the value of an American education. Drive a cab, all of them. Working at night, all of them. Living in the house, fourteen or fifteen people, but all of them are working, and got their books with them. They're at the community college, they are over at junior college working their way [to the university]. And they are going to become doctors, lawyers, and engineers and our people, born here, are standing around watching people go by."

Cosby's words lead to a disturbing question. Why are so many black Americans, people born inside the gates of American opportunity, still living as if they were locked out from all America has to offer? The standard reply is that black Americans are strangers in their own land because of racial discrimination. The history of slavery, legal discrimination, and continuing negative stereotypes of black people is a blockade to black advancement. That is true. But it is also true that immigrants from Jamaica, Ethiopia, and Nigeria are black. And many of them find a way to succeed. It is definitely true that most black people born in the United States are no longer poor. The *Brown* decision opened doors that allowed most black Americans to climb into the middle class.

The critics charging racism in the botched New Orleans rescue effort didn't bother to mention it, but the black middle class in New Orleans was not affected by the helter-skelter madness of that city after the storm. The city's mayor, Ray Nagin, a successful black businessman, moved his family to Dallas. Regardless of race, people with cars, credit cards, bank accounts, family, and friends had a way out.

What the hurricane blew into the open was the subterranean life of New Orleans, the unusually deep-seated black poverty that tourists never see on their tours of the French Quarter, Mardi Gras, and antique stores. Some numbers help to tell the story.

In 2004, 23 percent of the all the people of New Orleans, black and white, lived in poverty, nearly double the national average of 12.7 percent. Thirty-eight percent of the city's children (people under eighteen) survive below the poverty level, again about double the national average of 17.8. It is also higher than the 34 percent of black children nationally who live in poverty.

Race and poverty are as close as red beans and rice in New Orleans, because about 70 percent of the city's residents are black—the blackest large city in the nation—and nine out of ten poor families in New Orleans are black. Overall, about 35 percent of the city's black population lives in poverty (higher than the national black poverty rate of about 25 percent). Even among black people who have jobs in New Orleans, more than one-third remain stuck in poverty because of low-paying positions such as kitchen help and janitors.

The 2004 poverty line, as defined by the Census Bureau, stood at about $9,600 for one person and about $19,300 for a family of four. New Orleans has the most concentrated black poverty of any American city.

Dr. Silas Lee, an African American research analyst, found in a 2000 study that that 25 percent of black New Orleans residents lived on less than $10,000 a year and more than 70 percent lived on less than $35,000.

The racial divisions in New Orleans are heightened by this intense black poverty, since 56 percent of whites in the city have incomes over $35,000, and 40 percent have incomes over $50,000. The poverty in New Orleans's black community also extends to a lack of education. One-third of black people in the city never finished high school. And when the hurricane started to rip away the pretty facade of "Big Easy" life, the poverty among black folks was revealed for all to see. Thirty-five percent of black New Orleans residents had no car or truck to take them away from the impending disaster.

New Orleans's extreme picture of poverty fits the profile of the South, which is the poorest area of the nation. For the years 2002 to 2004, Louisiana, with its poverty concentrated in New Orleans, was the fourth most impoverished state in the nation, falling just behind its neighbors, Mississippi and Arkansas.

New Orleans's historic ties to slave labor in the Mississippi Delta region and its abysmally high poverty level combined like the perfect storm to create the disturbing sight of so many poor black people scraping and scurrying to escape the flooding. Even President Bush, who rarely engages racial issues, said the high rate of poverty among blacks in the Gulf Coast "has roots in a history of racial discrimination which cut off generations from the opportunity of America." Sad pictures of poor people, mostly black, holding plastic trash bags with all their belongings above waist-deep flood waters created a national discussion about the persistence of poverty in America. Census numbers indicated that poverty has been on the rise beginning in 2000, despite a general economic recovery. The recovery boosted stocks and paychecks for well-educated

Americans. But if you don't own stocks, if you work at a low-wage job, or if you were out of work, the recovery did nothing for you. And, disproportionately, black Americans don't have stocks and don't hold highly paid jobs. They have also consistently faced an unemployment rate twice of white Americans.

The race and class divide is not as sharp around the country as it is in New Orleans, but the nationwide poverty rate for black Americans is twice the national poverty rate. As a result, the concern in black America over poor people is much higher than it is in white America. With one-quarter of black people living in poverty, it is more likely for any black man or woman to come in contact with neighbors, friends, or a relative who is struggling with poverty. And even middle-class black Americans don't have the savings and investments of white Americans.

The split between Americans familiar with poor people, and Americans who don't know poor people, as well as the split between people with big bank accounts and people with no money in the bank, leads black and white Americans to split their opinions on how the federal government handled Hurricane Katrina.

For example, 77 percent of white Americans said the government would have been just as unprepared to deal with the hurricane if the city was mostly white. The whites polled also said rescue efforts would have been just as slow even if wealthy white people had been stranded. About 70 percent of whites said race and poverty did not affect the government's inept response to the disaster on the Gulf Coast. Black people expressed a markedly different view. Seventy-one percent of black people, in an ABC News poll, said authorities would have done a better job of flood protection and emergency preparation if New Orleans were not predominantly black and poor. An overwhelming number of blacks, 76 percent, told the pollster the government would have been faster to respond if the faces on TV had been rich white people. And 63 percent of black Americans (with only 25 percent of whites in agreement) said problems with hurricane relief efforts indicated continued racial inequality in America.

Harry Belafonte told an audience of black people at the 2005 Congressional Black Caucus conference in Washington, D.C., that no probe into the government's failed response was necessary because "we know what caused it": racism. Charles Rangel, the Harlem congressman and senior black leader in Congress, said that President "Bush is our Bull Connor" (a reference to the notorious Birmingham, Alabama, police chief). Harvard University law professor Lani Guinier said the government's lack of urgency was more proof that in modern America "poor black people are the throwaway people." Kanye West, the rapper, bluntly said that the bumbling government response came about because the Republican president George Bush "doesn't care about black people."

The racial divide about the reason for the government's ineptitude became big news. It fit the old news formula of black and white people as opposites, seeing a different America. Unfortunately, that facile conclusion obscured a larger reality that is critically important. In a Pew poll taken after Katrina, most black Americans (56 percent) agreed with an overwhelming majority of white Americans (77 percent) that in recent years the position of black Americans has improved. In fact, it is really telling that two-thirds of black Americans (66 percent) and a nearly identical percentage of white Americans (71 percent) are concerned that too many poor people are overly dependent on the government to live. These trends go back as far as 2003. The same poll found that 43 percent of black Americans say that black people who are not moving ahead are causing their own problems, and 63 percent of whites agree.

These poll respondents are Cosby's amen corner, even if they don't stand up at a public gala event at Constitution Hall and say the poor and working class in black America are "not holding their end in this deal."

The rock-solid support for Cosby's views is evident when people are asked by the pollsters if "individuals have it in their own power to succeed." There is no debate: 70 percent of white Americans say yes, and 62 percent of black Americans agree that hard work leads to success. Some white people may be dismissed as naive to the realities of race given their conviction that hard-working people, no matter their color, can make a go of it in modern America. But how can anyone dismiss the fact that most black people agree. That sounds like all of America is picking up on Bill Cosby's challenge that too many poor and low-income black people are not taking advantage of opportunities to get themselves out of poverty.

This overwhelming agreement that individuals, including poor black people, can make their way up the economic ladder is hidden in black America at the moment because of anger at President Bush. Bad-mouthing the president is not going to get much argument in black America, where more than 90 percent of black people have voted against President Bush in the last two presidential elections. And the finger-pointing at the conservative man in charge is surely to be appreciated among black people as a smart, strategic political attempt to stir what little remains of the white racial guilt that led to antipoverty programs in the 1960s. All of those facts added to the deep emotional upset of black Americans at seeing so many poor black people unable to help themselves. It was impossible for any politically conscious black American not to identify with the black people struggling for the basics of life in the aftermath of Katrina. That led to high sensitivity over any word or action that focused on race. Before blasting the president for not caring enough about black people, Kanye West, the rapper, expressed the pain of always seeing black people as a bedraggled lot. "I hate the way they portray us in the media," he said on a TV broadcast from the "Concert for Hurricane Relief."

West wasn't the only one upset at the down and desperate pictures of black folks. Overly sensational reporting about rumors of murder and rape among the poor black people at New Orleans shelters added to the discomfort. And there was political pressure, too. White conservative commentators played to stereotypes of black criminality to counter stories focused on the government's failure to offer emergency help to people in need. "All you see on TV is African Americans looting," said a black woman quoted in the *Baltimore Sun*. "They portray them in a negative light. But if people are desperate—black, white, yellow, green, they are going to seek what they can find." Keith Woods, dean of the Poynter Institute, a media studies group, said black Americans feared the racial fallout of whites watching TV coverage that played to every negative racial stereotype of poor blacks in a moment of crisis. "We stop seeing the blackness of the rescue worker," he said. "We see only the blackness of the hoodlums. We stop seeing the whiteness of the refugees, and we only see the whiteness of the helpers."

Two black women wrote in the *Washington Post* that stories about gangs of black rapists in storm-ravaged New Orleans reminded them of the history of scary, racist images used to vilify Chinese and German immigrants, as well as blacks, in the Galveston Hurricane of 1900 and the San Francisco earthquake of 1906. The immigrants and blacks "were rumored to be preying on white women by chewing on their fingers to steal their jewelry. It's not such a stretch to see parallels in the unconfirmed reports of roving bands of rapists in New Orleans." In Utah the state's attorney general, Mark Shurtleff, justified those fears when he repeated an outright lie. He said "several dozen" black people fleeing from the storm and brought to Utah were "convicted murderers." He later apologized for passing on bad information, but the strong racist overtones—why were evacuated black people having their criminal records checked, and were whites also being subjected to this kind of review?—added to the feeling that all black people were being demonized because of news coverage that associated poverty and crime with black skin.

The anxiety in black America was evident when complaints showered TV and newspaper correspondents who referred to the poor black people left behind as "refugees." Civil rights leaders argued that "refugees" sounded as if these poor souls had crossed the border from another country. They insisted that the people left behind to face the worst of the storm were Americans and deserved the American government's help. The same prickly response from black America erupted again when whites appearing in pictures on the Internet, wading through floodwaters with loaves of bread in their hands, were described as "carrying" food, while the caption on a picture of black people holding food described them as "looters."

This major psychic discomfort in black America took a turn to the paranoid when the Nation of Islam's leader, Louis Farrakhan, suggested that the levees had been intentionally destroyed by the government with bombs as an attack on poor black neighborhoods. "The divers went down under [the levees]," Farrakhan told a group in Memphis. "They took a chunk of some of the concrete . . . because there were burn marks on that concrete that suggested two different types of explosives. And these explosives are from the government side." Farrakhan's words sent conspiracy theories floating around talk shows and on the Internet. Several days later, when a TV interviewer asked the minister if he had any evidence of the government bombing the levees, he backed away: "Now, I don't know whether it did or did not happen, but when people believe something like that, it is the duty of those who can search out a rumor and prove its truth or its falsehood."

That drew a sharp response from black conservatives. Ward Connerly, who gained fame for opposing affirmative-action plans, said too many black people find it easy to blame the government because "they are looking for someone to blame." He added, "They can't blame God, so they're going to blame the government, the president, or racism. So many blacks have been conditioned to view everything through the prism of race that it's easy to come to that conclusion. But for the black leaders who are blaming racism, shame on them."

The battle between far-left conspiracy theories and the far-right outrage over black criminals was predictable and predictably not very enlightening. It is a failure of leadership on racial issues that is repeated time after time when a racial crisis erupts. But when serious people discussed the cause for the government's laconic and deficient response to the hurricane, the claims of racism proved to be weak, almost pathetic. Congressman Mel Watt, a North Carolina Democrat who is chairman of the Congressional Black Caucus, asked directly by the *Washington Post* if race was the cause of the slow government response, replied, "No, I don't believe that. I don't believe I can responsibly say that." Condoleezza Rice, the secretary of state and the top-ranking African American in the Bush administration, who was in meetings about the problem-plagued government response to the storm, rejected the racism charge as "poisonous." When she was asked about the charge that the Bush administration had acted slowly because so many black people were the victims, she said flatly, "What evidence is there that this is the case? Why would you say such a thing?" Ray Nagin, the mayor of New Orleans and a black man, told the ABC News program *Nightline* that it was not clear to him that race was the reason for so many poor blacks being caught in the floodwaters, "but it's a class issue for sure." Colin Powell, the former secretary of state, and according to polls one of the most admired Americans of any color, explained that what happened in New Orleans was the result of "poverty [that] disproportionately affects African Americans in this country. And it happened because they were poor."

Senator Barack Obama, an Illinois Democrat who is the only African American in the Senate, monitored the situation closely. He concluded, "The incompetence [by the federal government in helping Katrina's victims] was colorblind." Carl Brasseaux, director of the Center for Louisiana Studies, who had a firsthand look at the aftermath of the hurricane, said, "I don't think that race was the fundamental issue here." And a leading white Democrat from Louisiana, former senator John Breaux, got very specific in taking apart the charge that the Bush administration performed its rescue efforts so badly because of the color of the people in harm's way. "The two parishes south of New Orleans, St. Bernard and Plaquemines, are mostly white," said Breaux. "They are devastated and they arguably got a lot less attention than New Orleans."

Further evidence that racism was not the cause for the government's inept handling of the hurricane came from later data released by the state of Louisiana. The head of Louisiana Population Data Center, Joachim Singelmann, said the numbers showed black and white residents of the city, rich and poor, suffered death and damage in proportion to their presence in the city. While about half of the people killed by the storm and flooding were in poor neighborhoods, the other half were in middle-class and even wealthy areas of the city. "The fascinating thing is that it is so spread out," Singelmann told the *Los Angeles Times*. "It is not just the Lower Ninth Ward [a mostly poor and black area] . . . It is across the board, including some well-to-do neighborhoods." According to the state data, the *Times* wrote, 28 percent of the population in New Orleans is white, but 33 percent of the dead were white. The *Detroit Free Press* also did away with the myth that most of the people who died did not have cars to flee the storm. Four months after the storm, the newspaper reported: "At many addresses where the dead were found, their cars remained in their driveways, flood-ruined symbols of fatal miscalculation."

As the emotionally charged claims of racism faded for lack of proof, the debate shifted to why there are so many black people in poverty, both in New Orleans and the nation. And that brought the conversation back to Bill Cosby's controversial comments about poor black people who are not doing enough to take advantage of the opportunities opened up by the civil rights movement.

This is the debate that most Americans, black and white, wanted to hear because most Americans believe that if you want out of poverty in the early twenty-first century, you can get out of poverty. Americans are not pointing at the government and insisting on added spending on welfare and poverty programs unless it is going to help people get out of poverty. The 1996 welfare reform, designed under President Bill Clinton who is hugely popular with black Americans, was called the "Personal Responsibility and Work Opportunity Reconciliation Act." The heart of the legislation was aimed at getting people off welfare by linking welfare to job training. It succeeded in getting more than 9 million women and children out of the welfare system. Similarly, President Clinton was behind passage of another law, the Earned Income tax credit, to help people working low-paying jobs to stay above the poverty line.

The bottom line to the tax credit is that it makes getting up and going to work more rewarding than living on welfare. In combination with a hot economy during the 1990s, welfare reform and tax credits for the working poor got more than 4 million working-class people out of poverty. All of the legislation was put in place by a president with close ties to civil rights groups and black voters, and it did not cost him any of his support among black voters.

Ironically, white conservatives had the same idea. President Clinton was playing to the broad political middle that included conservatives by making welfare a program to get people back to work. The two-term president perceived that Americans wanted to help the poor, but not if it meant a steady diet of welfare that would leave people waiting for a government check. As the nation's most popular TV talk-show host, conservative Bill O'Reilly told one guest, "So the white American taxpayers are saying, 'How much more do we have to give here,' when in forty years of Great Society programs the poverty levels come down a little bit but not a lot. And 75 percent of those poor in the U.S. are white."

So we have two-thirds of black people and even more white people in agreement that it is debilitating for poor people of any color to be addicted to welfare and dependent on government. In an interview with this author, Bill Cosby agreed, saying it was damaging to black America when the government, without proper thought, spews out checks to all unmarried women with babies. Political voices from President Clinton to Bill O'Reilly have been expressing this same point for more than a decade. And then Bill Cosby breaks through the hard lines around the debate. He creates an opening for black America to say to poor black people that it is time to throw off the culture of poverty and take inspiration from a history of black sacrifice aimed at opening doors for future generations of black people. Cosby was not blaming anyone. He was asking people to focus on proven steps out of poverty—specifically getting a good education, getting married, and being good parents.

But instead of following in Cosby's footsteps, civil rights leaders ran for cover out of fear that angry black voices on the far left might say they had lost touch with poor black people and were no longer authentically black. Out of cowardice, they preferred to avoid the risk of stepping out and speaking the truth. Instead, they stayed in the safety of acceptable black public commentary by finding a target that most black Americans could agree to demonize—President Bush.

This is not to excuse the president and pretend that Bush and his fellow conservatives are in the forefront of the battle to eradicate poverty in America. "It is clear that the administration has not had [black and poor people] as high on their priority list as they should have," said Bruce Gordon, the head of the NAACP. Black leaders joined Democratic leaders in Congress in complaining about Republican plans to repeal the estate tax, a tax on the very wealthy that would take $745 billion out of the government's treasury in the ten years beginning in 2012. That proposed tax cut—which was tabled after Katrina—would have added to billions in previous tax cuts that went to the wealthiest Americans and built a record government deficit. California congresswoman Maxine Waters, a Democrat, highlighted the open wallet the Republicans in Congress offered to help survivors of the terrorist attacks on September 11, 2001. She contrasted that generosity with the cool reception the GOP-led Congress extended to spending on hurricane disaster relief involving a high percentage of blacks. Representative Waters told National Public Radio that "these right-wing Republicans are not going to get up off of this money easily," to help hurricane survivors because of the deficits created by President Bush. "This president has been spending like a . . . drunken sailor and now they all of a sudden want to get more conservative on the spending when we are talking about what we can do make those people whole and to rebuild New Orleans."

Senator Obama, the Illinois Democrat who had the heart to show some leadership by saying that, contrary to popular black opinion, racism was not the cause of the slow efforts to rescue the hurricane victims, found that he could stand with mainstream black opinion on this point. He told NPR: "Somebody once said that a government is about making choices and the choices that we've been making over the last four or five years have resulted in higher poverty rates . . . record numbers of people uninsured. That's not the kind of America that I think any of us want."

A Johns Hopkins University sociologist, Andrew Cherlin, said that while most Americans think the poor could do more to help themselves, the hurricane was "a case where the poor were clearly not at fault [for their predicament]." Speaking to *Newsweek*, he said it "was a reminder that we have a moral obligation to provide every American with a decent life."

As the consensus grew that what happened in New Orleans was a class issue, discussion of the storm and the plight of poor people left behind in the floodwaters led to criticism of the press and the government for ignoring the poor and not doing enough to help poor people, be they poor whites or poor blacks. It was reminiscent of the 1960s, when the sociologist Michael Harrington wrote *The Other America*, a book that spurred the federal government into a War on Poverty with programs such as Model Cities, Medicare, and Head Start. The hurricane also came at a time of a widening class divide in the nation. Several newspapers, from the *Wall Street Journal* to the *New York Times*, had recently run stories on growing disparities in health insurance, housing, and even income. According to the reports, the top 1 percent of the nation's workers now earned more in pre-tax income than the entire bottom 40 percent of American workers. The top 1 percent of households also held more wealth than the bottom 90 percent of American households. That economic problem affected more white people than black people. But because the hurricane put a black face on poverty, race became the center of all discussions of income inequality and poverty in America.

Somehow, though, the conversation never got around to steps the poor could take to help themselves. Without hesitation the conversation settled on what the government had to do to help the poor. Any discussion of how the poor failed to help themselves climb up the ladder of economic opportunity was reflexively dismissed as blaming the poor.

In that political framework, Cosby's call for poor black people to do more to help themselves put him on the side of the conservatives. The moment he finished his speech at the *Brown* commemoration, he was charged with giving support to enemies of black America. Theodore Shaw, head of the NAACP Legal Defense and Educational Fund, said he instantly knew Cosby's comments would be "hijacked by those who pretend that racism is no longer an issue and view poor black people with disdain." Shaw said it was predictable that "conservatives are applauding Bill Cosby for saying that the problems of the black community stem primarily from personal failures and moral shortcomings."

To Cosby, Shaw and the other critics are the "phonies." Speaking to this author, Cosby said: "Teddy's problem is he is afraid he is going to lose the white man's money. He told me, 'Hey, man, the economy has the white man's money drying up.' I want to know how you can be sincere to the cause of black people when the white man is drying up your check. I offered to help him. I said I'd be glad to put on a benefit performance, 'An Evening with Bill Cosby,' and I never heard from him. I guess he is mad because I told him, 'Ted, stand up and talk. Say Bill Cosby said this, and this is what I'm trying to do to fix the problem.' Never heard from him."

To Shaw and his fellow civil rights leaders, Cosby's words had the impact of giving the media, government, and corporations a free pass to avoid dealing with poverty, especially among minorities.

The media was widely criticized after Katrina for ignoring the poor unless there was a riot such as those that occurred in L.A. in 1992, after a black man, Rodney King, was videotaped being beaten by police. Debate over poverty faded into oblivion in the political arena after the Clinton welfare reform debate of the mid-1990s.

President Bush did not have an antipoverty program. His administration focused on the middle class by encouraging what he called an "Ownership Society," a policy of increasing home ownership, individual ownership of health insurance plans, private ownership of social security investments, and student ownership of vouchers that allowed any child in a failing school to go to a better school. To deal with the poor, the Bush administration's Faith Based Initiative pushed to funnel money to churches to allow religious principles, instead of government policy, to guide efforts to help poor people, be they homeless, hungry, or jobless. As for blacks and Hispanics, President Bush's policy encouraged more small-business loans and more diversity in hiring, as exemplified by his record of hiring a record number of black cabinet officials. These steps had the potential to help the black and Hispanic middle class, but ignored poor people. The Bush administration also opposed increases in the minimum wage.

The Democrats did not have any policies for helping the poor, either. During the 2004 presidential election, the issue of poverty was not addressed. The most powerful speech of that campaign season was about the growing class divide in America. The Democrats' vice-presidential candidate, John Edwards, delivered his "Two Americas" speech to widespread acclaim. But the speech said almost nothing about the poor. Edwards lamented the problems of a growing number of middle-class Americans, especially people who had worked in industries and lost jobs because

U.S. firms moved their manufacturing facilities overseas to find cheaper labor. He expressed regret at the lost bargaining power of unions. Those workers found themselves forgotten in a global economy, losing ground, even losing their health insurance, as the ranks of the rich and the upper middle class grew. Edwards spoke with sincere regret at older people facing the high cost of prescription drugs and the increasing cost of home heating fuel and gas. To appeal to black voters, he also talked about the need for continued support of affirmative action, but affirmative action helps minorities and women with education, skills, and résumés. It does little for the unskilled people of color who are poor. Edwards also spoke with feeling about the shame of bad public schools in the big cities, but, like Democrats in Congress, he did not have any strong ideas for fixing those schools. At best he criticized the Bush administration's "No Child Left Behind" plan for its focus on testing, but he trailed off into rhetorical attacks because he had no strong prescription for his own cure.

The lack of consistent media attention and the absence of political will to deal with rising poverty in the nation add to the isolation and alienation of the poor, especially the minority poor. But it does point to the "compassion fatigue" that afflicts American politics, which makes it all the more important that the poor are empowered to fight for themselves. There is agreement across racial lines that the poor remain too dependent on government. Jodie Allen, a senior editor at the Pew Research Center for the People and the Press, wrote that Pew's polling of blacks and whites after Hurricane Katrina found a "striking congruence on a range of attitudes and opinion that have traditionally been viewed as central to the American creed." Looking through the Pew poll numbers, she discovered that even at a time of crisis, most black Americans "share the general belief in the benefits of hard work and are equally admiring of those who acquire wealth through it. . . . Two-thirds of blacks share the concern that too many low-income people are dependent on government aid." Allen was particularly impressed that two-thirds of black Americans and nearly three-quarters of white Americans agree that too many poor people are dependent on government aid.

The clear consensus among black and white Americans is that waiting on government programs to get out of poverty, relying on welfare checks and subsidies, can kill the human spirit. Government programs have built housing projects that concentrate poor people in decaying neighborhoods with a culture of poverty—drugs, crime, fatalism, and a lack of access to jobs and the larger culture of work. That is quicksand, pulling poor people under, suffocating them by not-so-subtly encouraging them to surrender any dream of getting into the economic mainstream of American life.

This is not a mean-spirited attitude. It is wisdom. Black people, just like white people, want the best for their children and friends. They want them to avoid the pitfalls evident to them after years of watching 1960s-era welfare policies that drove men out of the house and increased single-parent families, the most impoverished group in the nation. It is wisdom that comes from seeing what happens to families in which the discipline of hard work is undermined by a culture of people waiting for the next government program, which is often underfunded or eventually cut for lack of money. The Pew poll found that 62 percent of black Americans felt that the government controlled too much of daily life. As for government regulation and social programs, the polls found that blacks, as a whole, were "considerably more dubious about its efficacy than are whites; nearly half of black respondents say regulation of business does more harm than good."

Hurricane Katrina washed away illusions about waiting for even the mighty federal government to help anyone, including poor black people. The flooding revealed the wisdom that is at the heart of Bill Cosby's call for "the lower economic and lower middle economic people [to hold up] their end of the deal." People who don't take steps to hold themselves above the rising tide, to lift their families out of poverty, will find themselves sinking, if not drowning. Insisting that the government do its job is critical, but to depend so completely on others to care for your basic needs is suicidal. Bill Cosby took the risk of going into the political high waters to ask why so many black people remain mired in poverty. Why is the hard core of those in poverty, especially the so-called Black Underclass, so hard to raise up, even after fifty years of newly opened doors in the wake of the *Brown* decision and a mighty civil rights movement?

Hurricane-strength winds revealed the shocking number of lost souls, trapped by poverty and unable to save themselves in a crisis. But instead of seeing this as a sign from the gods that new ideas have to be embraced, the critics closed their eyes to any prophetic message in Katrina's wrath. Those are the same critics who condemn Bill Cosby, condemn the black middle class, condemn the Bush administration, and lash out at conservative opponents of social programs. Not one of those critics offers any reply to the question that flows naturally from people who truly want to help the poor: How do we help the poor get out of poverty?

Cosby's answers were plain and obvious: Take care about when you have sex, when you get pregnant, and be sure to graduate from school. His answer is also to do a better job of parenting once a child is born, including putting more money into education than into consumer goods. Cosby also calls for neighborhoods to come together, to organize against criminals and drug addicts. Although spoken by an entertainer, these are prophetic calls to the poor and the powerless. Here is a flood of truth, a real rising tide, to lift to safety any soul willing to listen to the warnings and prepare his or her boat for the coming storm.

9

THE COSBY SHOW

ALMOST A YEAR TO the day after his May 17, 2004, speech in Washington, Bill Cosby is on stage in Houston. His celebrity attracted another full house for one of the free town-hall meetings he has held in poor black neighborhoods since saying that today's poor people are not "holding up" their end of the long fight for equal rights. James Campbell, an editorial writer for the *Houston Chronicle*, introduces Cosby as a man in pain, a man who grimaced when he whispered privately to Campbell that all he is trying to do is give black people a "wake-up call."

The audience gives Cosby a standing ovation as he comes onstage wearing dark glasses. A year has passed, but Cosby, who has never apologized for what he said in Washington, is still on fire. He starts out telling people not to wait for any more government programs to lift them out of poverty. "How many government programs have you waited for and when they arrived nothing happened?" How far downhill will public schools have to go before you "realize that you have to do something?" he shouts. The funnyman is in no mood for laughs tonight. He tells the mostly black audience they've been abandoned by a government that "took you from your homeland to build a better place . . . for them."

There is an edge to this humor. It is not like Cosby. He is going somewhere with this. Something seems to be bothering him. Now the hurt that critics have laid on Cosby starts to show, even with the shades covering his eyes. Not two minutes into this speech, he gets highly defensive.

"I'm not denying systemic racism," he explains, striking out at all the civil rights leaders and intellectuals who say he is closing his eyes to the power of a racist system. "I'm not denying that [systemic racism], never have. I've lived it. I don't need to show you a card about what has happened to me."

Then he does a U-turn. Cosby connects attempts to make him a pariah in the black community with his earlier riff about the history of the government abandoning black people. The souls of black Americans have long been abandoned, he begins. Black people are taught not to believe in themselves, told they can't be the hero in the movie. He talks about children being abandoned. They are abandoned by being left at risk in neighborhoods where there is gunfire; they are abandoned in declining schools; they are abandoned at home because parents are absent. Suddenly, Cosby returns to his experience of being abandoned after speaking out. He is talking back to the critics.

"You don't tell me that I've made a lot of money and I've become a multimillionaire and I forgot where I came from," he cries out as the crowd begins to give him sustained applause. "You don't tell me I'm a billionaire who's making fun of poor people. If I didn't like you, I wouldn't say a damned thing."

Now the audience is giving Cosby a standing ovation.

"I mean, isn't that fair? If I didn't love you, I'd say, 'Keep on doing what you're doing, you're doing just fine . . .' and next year

I'd see eighty-six percent of you dropping out of school, 'cause you are doing a wonderful job."

The audience, still standing, is now laughing and clapping.

"But if I love, if I love you, I'm crying, I'm in pain," he says, and now the audience is giving up "amen" and "hmm-hmm." It is call-and-response, a church testimonial, a prophet coming in from the wilderness.

Houston was an unusual performance for Cosby. At most of his appearances he is all business and does not open up. In Houston, however, he got very personal. He allowed everyone in the room to see the scars from all the backstabbing and cutting remarks.

There was a glimpse of the pain a few weeks earlier in Springfield, Massachusetts, where he told a big crowd not to be taken in by his critics. "Please don't let some fool sell you [that] 'Bill Cosby doesn't like people,'" he said. "I'm talking about all these fakes, and you know who they are. All these fakes and the people who are propping them up and taking a little cut [of the government money for poverty programs]."

At an event in Pittsburgh, he cut through the pain and defended himself by calling on black legends: "You teach your child that this message that is coming today with Bill Cosby . . . teach your child that Malcolm X said it forty-two years ago! Marcus Garvey said it some sixty or seventy years ago! DuBois said it! Bethune said it! Education."

These bursts of anger at his critics opened the curtains on Cosby's true feelings about the intense pressure on him once he took a leap into a sharp, fast-spinning debate about race, class, and politics in black America.

Immediately after his *Brown* anniversary speech, he seemed surprised by the heated reaction to what he said. He got some support, but the most passionate response was damning. The loud voices of critics got amplified because the TV shows and radio talk shows all wanted to peek behind the closed doors of enforced black unity in any discussion of the current state of the black community. The rule among the leading voices in racial discussions is to sing from the same hymnal, even if a change in seasons brings new ideas, issues, and personalities. Black America has seen tremendous development in the last fifty years, but the official message from civil rights leaders remains the same: Black people are victims of the system, and the government needs to increase social spending. In addition, even the most dysfunctional and criminal behavior among black people is not to be criticized by black leaders. On the contrary, it is to be denied and hidden in the name of protecting the image of blacks as disadvantaged, oppressed, and perpetually victimized. Anyone who breaks with that official message is accused of being an Uncle Tom and a sellout.

So, when Cosby sang a different song, with lyrics long heard in private among black people but never from black leaders, the media was not interested in his call for attention to a crisis of school dropouts, black people in jail, and births to single mothers. The real news to the reporters was simply that Cosby had gone off the reservation. The news shows wanted to see the real dogfight backstage as steps were taken to stop anyone else from breaking ranks. The media was egging on the fight. As a result, any critic who said Cosby was attacking poor black people got a microphone. Anyone who claimed to be a spokesman for "the people," standing up to a bullying billionaire, could get on the air.

Cosby's initial response was defensive and private. He was not going to knuckle under to bullying, or add credibility to the critics by going head-to-head with them. He later gave the *L.A. Times* his private assessment of his critics: "What they are yelling about has to do with the pain that comes with having the covers pulled off and responsibility put in its proper place."

In public, Cosby's response was to blame the *Washington Post*'s coverage of the speech. As talk shows and newspapers around the nation picked up the *Post*'s reporting—usually excerpts of the most sensational quotes—Cosby had his agent, David Brokaw, issue a statement condemning "media rumors" that he had turned against poor black people. The statement said that the *Post* story, first run as an item in their gossip column, "Reliable Sources," "left out an important piece of information." The gossip column failed to write, the Brokaw Company explained, that Cosby was speaking out of concern over the "epidemic" of black children dropping out of school. "The *Post* article inaccurately character- ized Cosby's remarks as a general criticism of the black lower eco- nomic classes," the press release said. "Mr. Cosby explains that his comments were intended to be a call to action, a plea to 'turn the mirror around on ourselves.'"

The lengthy statement revealed a Cosby who was stunned at the negative response. His message was not being given a fair hearing. He was not supported by other prominent black people. He was alone.

No offer to advance his message came from the NAACP, the Urban League, the Congressional Black Caucus, the churches, or the major black colleges and universities. No one picked up on his call for marches against teen pregnancy and dropping out of school. Cosby told this author that several black leaders, such as former Atlanta Mayor Andy Young, had told him in private that he was right. But Young and the others did not offer to stand by his side and offer a full-throated defense. He was told they didn't want to "be thought of as old fuddy-duddies."

"You know hip-hop and *The Boondocks* established that older black people are not to be taken seriously," he said in the inter- view. "Even if Andy Young and Julian Bond [the NAACP chairman] speak out, if you don't know who they are, if you don't know history it doesn't make any difference to you. And these people don't know history, they don't know about who faced down bigots to help them. This stuff is so big that Andy and Julian feel they can't stop it."

Cosby intended to be a catalyst for change. He wanted his daring words to set the stage for a new era of civil rights activism aimed at strengthening black America through stronger families, better education, and a can-do, self-reliant attitude that rejected the view of black people as weaklings waiting for somebody else to save them.

The support never materialized. Instead, Cosby felt he was being subjected to personal attacks by people who did not want to talk about the substance of his remarks. In place of attention to the crisis of school dropouts and teen pregnancy in black America, Cosby told me, his critics found it easier to defame Bill Cosby. The critics scolded him for being "accidentally black," throughout his career as a comedian and actor. They said his lack of public rage over racism made white Americans comfortable with the status quo and allowed them to justify neglecting the poor. The critics also said Cosby was guilty of condescending to black people, being too old, too bourgeois, and part of a history of middle-class black people being ashamed of the black poor. They said he was too much of an integrationist, a man who created "color-blind" comedy that highlighted "human oneness and clinging to the universal 'whiteness.'" The charge against Cosby was that his push to bring black people into that "human oneness" made him an enemy of an authentically black point of view of American life.

Michael Eric Dyson, in his book *Is Bill Cosby Right? (Or Has the Black Middle Class Lost Its Mind?)*, wrote, "I think it is Cosby's embarrassment for the poor in the sight of the 'White Man' that has caused him to go off on the poor."

Cosby felt contempt for his critics. "These people aren't bringing anything to the table but a dislike for Bill Cosby," he said. In a later interview, Cosby added that as the criticism mounted he felt very alone: "What saddens me is that intellectuals, educators, and writers are afraid to say this is not making any sense . . . that [my critics] are leading our children into the valley of death."

He had never experienced this kind of public rebuke. For most of his career he has been so lovable and lacking in controversy that major advertisers, from Jell-O to Kodak, selected his smiling face and wide eyes to sell their products. And it was unmistakably a black face. He is to this day a one-man band for integration and racial equality in American popular culture. Cosby is still viewed as a crossover star, a hero to people of all races and yet acknowledged as a man who celebrated his blackness. He has a place at the table with black leadership going back to the 1960s, when he emerged as one of the first black TV stars, in the series *I Spy*.

The crusade to improve the image of black America in popular culture has been at the heart of Cosby's art since he arrived in Hollywood. On the sets of his shows, he took a decrease in profits to create apprenticeships for black people trying to get their union cards so they could break into the film and TV industries as set designers, camera operators, makeup artists, and more.

On the air, Cosby shaped decidedly healthy images of black people on TV, turning away from the *Amos 'n' Andy* minstrel-show portrayal of the race. His television work created strong, successful, and self-reliant images of blackness. It landed a direct hit against the negative cultural typecasting of black people as ignorant and lazy that had persisted since the days of *Birth of a Nation*. His books, such as *Fatherhood*, became national best-sellers among people of all races. He proved that a mass market could cross racial lines to buy the non-stereotypical image of a black family with love, good parenting, and good values. Cosby's contribution was a key part of a historic transformation of black identity in America in the late twentieth century, as the black middle class grew in numbers and political power. Cosby was in the middle of that success.

His series in the 1980s, *The Cosby Show* and *A Different World*, both celebrated strong black families and the value of education. Over half of the TV sets in use during the half-hour time slot for *The Cosby Show* were tuned to that one show. It is a record performance with tremendous, positive impact on American race relations. Just the publicity he gave to black colleges created a renaissance for those schools as applications and financial contributions both increased. And it is no stretch to say that Cosby made college education attractive to many young black people who might not have had a vision of going to school.

When Cosby was inducted into the Hall of Fame for the Academy of Television Arts and Sciences in 1992, he didn't simply say "thank you," but spoke passionately about the need for TV writers, producers, and actors to portray black Americans as real people. He said too many TV writers were guilty of "drive-by" scenes that come from driving by black people who are standing on a corner and imagining those people as representative of all black America. He charged that too many television executives still regretted that *Amos 'n' Andy*, with its broad stereotypes of sly, stupid black people, was off the air. He asked why TV had so few images of black people who went to college and worked hard and loved their families. "Stop this horrible massacre of images that are being put on the screen now," he said. "It isn't fair. It isn't fair to your [white] children watching. Because that isn't us. It isn't us."

After Dr. King's assassination, he became a major supporter of

Jesse Jackson's Operation Breadbasket. He has raised millions of dollars by putting on benefit performances at which all money goes to nonprofits and civil rights groups. In 1986 he gave "every cent" from a million-dollar contract with Kodak to black colleges at a time when schools such as Fisk University faced financial crisis. In 1987 he donated more money, $1.3 million, to Shaw, Florida A&M, Howard, and Central State universities. He gave $750,000 to Bethune-Cookman College. On November 4, 1988, he and his wife, Camille, gave $20 million to Spelman College. He also gave Meharry Medical College $800,000. *Ebony* magazine called Cosby and his wife the "First Family of Philanthropy." Cosby has also been involved politically, giving financial support to the anti-apartheid movement in South Africa when the movement was being attacked as a communist front. He regularly supports black American political candidates, even controversial efforts such as the failed campaign by former Charlotte, North Carolina, mayor Harvey Gantt against Republican arch-conservative Jesse Helms. Cosby contributed to Gantt's campaign at a time when another black celebrity, North Carolina native Michael Jordan, opted to stay out of the fight instead of risking his standing with conservative white corporate sponsors. Jordan said he could not support the black Democrat because "Republicans buy shoes, too." Cosby took a risk that Jordan ducked.

Given his long history of improving black images in American media, major financial contributions to black colleges, and personal support for black politicians, Cosby reasonably expected to be taken seriously as he used his credibility to deliver a difficult message. He didn't anticipate being left to defend himself. In an interview more than a year after the controversy erupted, he is still clearly scarred. Cosby said he had had many private conversations over the years with leaders in civil rights, academia, and politics about the problems of the black poor. They agreed with his opinion about the self-defeating behavior among too many poor black people. By taking the risk of repeating those sentiments in public, he expected all of his friends to salute his honesty and his willingness to take the risk for what he felt was the greater good of black people, and stand with him in public. They didn't.

Cosby stood alone in the storm. He seemed to be pleading for someone to step out and help him. In the press release his agent issued during the first days of the uproar, he explained defensively that when he traveled to perform around the nation, he saw numerous stories of twelve-year-old children killed in drive-by shootings, and of young men who fathered children without taking responsibility for the children, and of young women with no jobs or education, having children while living with their mothers and grandmothers. "I think it's time for concerned African Americans to march, galvanize, and raise the awareness about this epidemic to transform our helplessness, frustration, and righteous indignation into a sense of shared responsibility and action."

His statement closed with a response to the charge that he was serving up negative images of poor black people as ammunition for right-wing talk shows and conservative politicians. "I feel I can no longer remain silent," Cosby said. "If I have to make a choice between keeping quiet so that conservative media does not speak negatively, or ringing the bell to galvanize those who want change in the lower economic community, then I choose to be a bell ringer."

After the release of the statement, Cosby pulled back, limiting appearances and turning down most requests for interviews, as he tried to study the situation. He absolutely stayed away from any conservative news outlets, out of fear that it might lend support to the argument that he was giving the right-wing ammunition to belittle black people.

He did keep a promise to appear at Jesse Jackson's Rainbow/

PUSH convention in Chicago. Jackson joined him on stage. It was just a month and a half after his Washington speech, and a clearly tense Cosby was gently asked by the moderator, Harvard law professor Charles Ogletree, to explain what was going through his mind when he decided to deliver such a controversial speech in front of the NAACP. Ogletree described Cosby's controversial speech in Washington as one that was delivered "off the cuff." Cosby acknowledged it was not·a written text. He then talked about black history, specifically the sacrifices made to create opportunities for all black people during the civil rights movement. He mentioned a little black girl who had to endure so much racial bitterness, so many death threats as she walked to school, that federal marshals had to provide her with a ring of protection. She did all that, he said, to integrate schools so that future generations of black children had a chance at a better education.

As he was answering the question, something clicked in his mind, and without being prompted, Cosby began to address his critics. It is a mistake to direct so much energy to blaming white people for the problems of the black poor, he said. "It is almost analgesic to talk about what the white man is doing against us," Cosby began. "It keeps a person frozen in their seat." When he spoke about the high dropout rate, he said, he was not talking about every black child in every school. "Ladies and gentlemen," he said, "I'm sorry, I was not talking about *all*. I just took it for granted that it would be understood . . . [that I] can't be talking about *all*."

He turned to the critics who said he was wrong to put down black American parents who "don't know a damned thing about Africa," but give their children names like "Shaniqua, Shaligua, Mohammed, and all that crap and all of them in·jail." When those words were repeated around the nation, they fell flat among black Americans who took pride in their African roots. In Chicago,

Cosby explained that all those African names mean strength and power, but few black parents raise their children to be powerful. He said he should have made that clear. "Now, am I talking about everybody? No, of course not," he said, as someone in the audience yelled out "Preach."

Next, he spoke to the critics who said he was wrong to make fun of black slang, especially since some of his comedy characters used it. Black people who have gone to school, started businesses, and supported families can use that language with friends, Cosby said. "There's nothing wrong with the pharmacist saying, 'So, wasssup.' And you say [in response] 'wassup' or whatever is up and you is 'upping.' But the pharmacist has to understand Latin and so does the doctor." The crowd offered loud applause in support, and some people yelled out "Yes!"

And finally he answered the critics who said he should not have made a critical speech at a celebration of the *Brown* decision, in front of the leaders of the NAACP. "If not in front of the [long pause] National [pause] Association [pause] of Colored [pause] People . . . where shall I speak?" Any hostility in the audience totally vanished. There was laughter. "I just hope you understand my passion . . . my love . . . my years of watching people march, people being punched in the face . . . dogs, water hoses that tear the bark off of trees, Emmett Till. And you are going to tell me you're going to drop out of school? You're going to tell me that you're going to steal from a store?"

Professor Ogletree lavished kind words on Cosby on stage. "Thank you, Reverend Cosby." But Ogletree's kid-glove treatment was hiding a hard-knuckled follow-up question. What about the black middle class's responsibility to "help lift up those who suffer?" he asked. Implicit in the question was another sharp edge of criticism. What about the black middle class keeping troubles with the black poor a private issue, something to be addressed inside the black community, instead of publicly engaging in potentially divisive discussions? A still wound-tight Cosby went off. "This is an epidemic," he said. "Fifty percent [dropout rate] . . . and people want to defend something as 'your dirty laundry.' Hey, man, let me tell you something. Your dirty laundry gets out of school at two-thirty every day."

The Rainbow/PUSH audience literally gasped. Then there was applause. Cosby was in full flight, unplugged and unleashed. "It's cursing and they're calling each other 'nigger' as they walk up the street. They think they're hip . . . they take it into the candy store . . . on the train and on the buses. And they don't care what color or what age somebody else is, it's about them and they're cursing and grabbing each other . . . beat up other children because they're studying. Beat up young girls because they're virgins. . . .

"Those of you [in the black middle class] who feel [you] don't want to speak up because [you will] be embarrassed . . . it's way past that. You've got to come out," he said, to more applause. He kept going, using Jesse Jackson's famous line that every black person is "somebody" to say everyone has a right to speak. As for black unity and black pride, he turned the question on its head. "Whatever happened to 'Black Is Beautiful?'" he asked. "Well, it was replaced with 'Nigger, please.'" The crowd went wide-eyed, then burst into applause and laughter.

After his appearance in Chicago, Cosby arranged to make free public appearances in cities with large populations of poor black people. Often he phoned black columnists, some of whom had criticized his speech, and asked them to help him set up a meeting. The newspaper often agreed to be the sponsor, and it was put on by a local poverty group, the local school system, or black college. Unlike his appearances in Chicago or Houston, Cosby generally did not spend a lot of time defending his comments about the black poor. He spoke about how poor people could get power in their lives by taking responsibility as parents and neighborhood leaders. He visited more than a dozen urban centers including Newark, St. Louis, Atlanta, Dallas, Cleveland, and Baltimore. The sessions had the feel of a revival meeting, or an inspirational rally with a famous self-help guru. He often presented himself as a magnet, drawing the attention of low-income people who felt alienated and did not pay attention to schoolteachers, ministers, policemen, or city officials. When the *St. Louis Post Dispatch* columnist Sylvester Brown introduced him in that city, he noted that Cosby didn't have to take the time and make the effort to be there. "Mr. Cosby's rent is paid," he said, eliciting loud laughter. At an event in Springfield, the mayor, Charles Ryan, was on stage. He said Cosby couldn't solve all problems, but he had prayed that Cosby would agree to come to Springfield because "you need a catalyst, you need somebody to get the ball rolling."

In an interview for this book, Cosby said he remains frustrated with critics who dismiss what he is saying by arguing that it has all been said before. "How can you admit to hearing these things before and not having acted . . . not doing anything?" he asked.

At every stop, Cosby directed his speech to parents. He dealt with parenting, right down to how to feed a child. "Now, let's talk about what you are feeding them in the morning," he began in Springfield. "They can't make it on a doughnut . . . no chocolate cake. They need protein; they don't need a Pepsi-Cola and a bag of potato chips."

He encourages parents to challenge the public schools to educate the children, and that begins with showing up for meetings with teachers. The state is not in the business of raising children, he tells the parents. "So, if your child needs a hug, the school can't do that." At one stop he said, "Your children are too important to wait for a Bill Cosby or somebody. . . . Stop looking for somebody to pour money into it [schools, neighborhoods], and do it yourselves. This is about your children."

He warns the adults not to wait for the Federal Communications Commission, a disc jockey, or anyone else to turn off music and videos full of sex, violence, and degrading images of black people. "That's not a program in your house . . . you shut that thing off . . . People too long are so dependent . . . and when you are dependent you are going to have to do what the person who is giving you says." He extends the idea to profanity that adults use in front of children. "Please, those of you who are cursing at your children at home . . . hmmm . . . those children hear those words. When you put on a record and that record is yelling 'nigger' this and 'nigger' that and . . . those children hear that." The applause washes over him.

In Compton, California, he asked for an audience limited to foster parents, grandparents raising children, and the children in those homes. Cosby introduced leaders of city agencies and community groups who could help them. He held a second session, open to everyone, to discuss the city's sky-high murder rate. The headline out of the general session was Cosby's call for the city to have a parade to celebrate its most famous children, Venus and Serena Williams. Cosby also noted that Compton was where the tennis players' half sister, Yetunde, was shot and killed. But why not celebrate the good, the success of two local children, the Williams sisters, who are still alive and a success? "How difficult is it for Compton to have a parade so that parents can bring their children and say, 'They're from here!'"

When he was given a prize in Pittsburgh to honor his attention to promoting good eating habits, he asked that the ceremony be held at a middle school with students in attendance. Onstage he made the case that good nutrition is key to good parenting. "When they go to school in the morning . . . if they eat sugar they are going to go to sleep, the attention span is gone. And so you wonder why at third grade the child is leaving [himself] behind . . . it is because of the diet."

In general, at these sessions Cosby takes on a persona that is warm and fatherly, even grandfatherly. He is introduced as Bill Cosby, but the character onstage has the feel of Heathcliff Huxtable, the loving dad he played on his hit TV show. His style is down-home and funny. He brings children onstage or asks them to stand. In Springfield, Massachusetts, he invited children onstage and asked the crowd to take a look at the young talent growing up in their hometown. Pointing at the children, he asked the crowd of parents, school officials, and poverty program leaders, "Are there any junkies in this crowd, are there any drug dealers here?" In Houston he asked ten- and eleven-year-olds to stand up in the audience. He asked, "Do you see any pimps here? Do you see any whores there? Do you see any lawyers there? Do you see any engineers there? Do you see any people who will be able to help this nation?"

Once the spotlight is focused on children, he goes directly to the theme of improving parenting among poor black adults. And he doesn't stop speaking about parenting throughout the speech. He makes a point of telling black fathers that their children need to see them. It is okay, he tells the men, to show up and hug your kids even if you have nothing more to offer. "I don't care if you don't have a job, that is not what the child cares [about]; I don't care if you are still on drugs, you straighten yourself up for a moment and you go and find your children, one by one, and you explain to them that Daddy is not well and he does understand that you need a hug . . . that's all I'm asking you males to do."

He talks candidly to low-income single mothers about the need to be aware of what their children see when they bring strange men into the house.

"I'm asking you mothers, you ladies without a man, we know you need a life, but be careful . . . if that man beats you up and leaves . . . be careful that your daughter may hear you while you are having sex. . . . We've got to respect these children," he preaches. He speaks about small facts of a parent's life. He tells them not to curse in front of their children because the children will start using the same words; he tells them to turn off vulgar music, on the radio or the TV; he tells them to say no to children who want to buy revealing clothes and clothes that make them look like convicts—do-rags on their heads and pants that fall so low that their underclothes are visible.

In Bill Cosby's neighborhood, parents tell children "No" when the girls dress with "clothes down to what you want to show," and boys strut around with their pants falling off like "they are halfway ready to have sex." That inappropriate dress is not style, Cosby says, but a message from children about how they live, about boys asking girls to have sex without a word about love or responsibility, "nothing about I care for you, nothing about may I go for a walk with you . . . just I'm hot, I'm leaking, I'm dripping, come on, and I know you want it, too . . . and you are going to raise your children to go for that kind of thing?"

On some trips he invites psychologists to join him. Cosby often speaks in psychological terms about the rejection felt by a boy or girl who doesn't know a father or feel the love of a mother. That failed parenting leads children to seek acceptance in gangs.

Those gangs, he says, will jump a man and "beat him and you see blood and you don't stop and why, because your father rejected you, you are killing your father." He talks in similar psychological terms about children without attentive, loving mothers. He often uses the word *abandoned* to describe how children feel when their parents are not hugging them, not disciplining them, and are not available to go to school to meet their teachers. In Cosby's opinion, these children suffer from low self-esteem, and that leads to behavioral problems and violence and drugs and self-hate. In his stories, black children hear from birth that they are at risk, challenged, and disadvantaged. That leads them to feel they are weak, helpless, worthless, he said. It leads them to give up in school and respond to corrupt leaders who are just trying to make a dollar off the problems of the poor. His concern that poor black people are psychologically twisted comes up time and again. He told one group, "We need psychiatrists out on the streets; we need ten tons of them out there."

Several times he spoke with sadness about the number of young black people in jail. Again he tied it to troubled psychologies, poor parenting, and neighbors who no longer watch what the children are up to. At a detention center the warden told him that more than 70 percent of the boys were prescribed depressants and other psychoactive drugs. When the boys get out, however, the warden said the medications are taken away. Cosby said that leads those boys to robbery, assault, and theft so they can drink alcohol, smoke marijuana, and snort cocaine to self-medicate. Those children are part of the reason, Cosby tells audiences, that black adults have come to fear the sight of black children on the streets.

The streets of black America often come into Cosby's talk. The streets are where children are shaped. And the power to change the fortunes of the poor is on those neighborhood streets. "We have to take it upon ourselves to build a power base," he told one group, "that nobody, not a politician, not a minister, not a rich person can get [to us] without coming through the neighborhood."

When he speaks about finding solutions to the social problems of poor black people, he begins with parenting and ends with neighborhoods. "The revolution is in the neighborhood," says Cosby. At another session he put it this way: "I'm telling you the answer is in the neighborhood . . . it is in the neighborhood, sitting right here. All you have to do is polish it and the *dis-* will fall off of that advantage." Speaking at another event he said, "The conversation is about our children, about our neighborhoods . . . it is about recognizing the power that exists within our communities and us, the power in us."

The storyteller in Cosby reminisces about a golden era of black neighborhoods when older people watched children and told parents what the children did, good and bad. The elderly did not fear the children, and freely disciplined any child who was out of line. Even the neighborhood wino would warn children to study so they didn't end up like him, begging and drinking liquor out of a bottle in a brown bag on the streetcorner. In Cosby's universe, the black neighborhood is a place where the schoolhouse, the church, the projects, and the corner store are full of love, full of caring people looking out for each other. They may not have the wealth of the suburbs, but they have the riches that come with a close community.

The values of that strong black community which nurtured children is being lost to parasites like drug dealers, Cosby tells his audiences.

"You don't see the drug dealer in the wealthy neighborhood, his car is not parked out there," Cosby begins, and then says he asks why the drug dealers don't hang out where the most money is to be found. "Why are they parked here, why are they shooting and killing here? There is no money here. Or is there? He turns you into an addict and now you are in the house stealing from your mother, stealing from your father."

These touchstones of children, family, schools, and neighborhoods in Cosby's presentations always get a positive response. The first "boo" has yet to be heard from a member of any of his audiences. The doors were open to all, and most of the people present were black people with low incomes.

When Cosby appeared in Chicago immediately after his controversial appearance in Washington, Jesse Jackson, his host, said that if a "right-winger, anti-black, hostile ideologue made the same statement, it'd be taken differently." Jackson said black "progressives" feared that the American press might use Cosby to talk about the lack of effort by black people, but not about the "opportunity deficit" caused by continued racism in the society. But he concluded that "if you're behind, you've got to run faster. And you may not be responsible for being down, but you must be responsible for getting up. . . . Bill is saying, 'Yes, let's fight the right fight, let's level the playing field, but drunk people can't do that, illiterate people can't do that.'"

Though he did not respond directly, after Jackson spoke, Cosby had a turn at the microphone and said that in all his talks in Washington and elsewhere, he was speaking to low-income blacks about what was best for them. He was not worried about the right-wingers or the racists. "I couldn't care less about what white people think about me at this time. If they want to take [my speech] and say things against my people, let them talk. . . . What are they doing to us that they're grandfathers didn't try to do to us? But what's different is what we are doing to ourselves."

Jackson's eventual support for Cosby was echoed by Princeton University professor Cornel West. Appearing on PBS, West said

Cosby's controversial remarks came from "great compassion and trying to get folks to get on the right track. We got some brothers and sisters who are not doing the right thing. . . . We know that Bill Cosby is not in the right wing. He's not Clarence Thomas. He is not Ward Connerly. We know him to be someone who over fifty years in his artistic career [has been] in deep solidarity with black people's struggle."

Cosby, on the same show, later said the politics didn't matter to him. Whether he followed right-wing politics or left-wing politics, he said, the fact remains that "some people are not parenting." Again, he made no apology.

A year later the ABC TV show *Nightline* did a program about Cosby's tour of poor black neighborhoods. The show opened with several quick interviews with black people on the streets of Philadelphia. What was so interesting about these man-on-the-street vignettes was the unanimity of opinion about Cosby.

"I agree with him one hundred percent," said the first woman to appear. "Our race is going to hell in a handbasket because people are not doing what they are supposed to do for their children."

A second unidentified person said, "He's not really blaming those who are down and out. What he's telling those who become down and out is 'Find a way to pull yourself up.'"

Another woman said, "I think this is just his way of calling us out."

The mayor of Philadelphia, John Street, said, "Cosby was clear. . . . They aren't going to get anyplace by not learning the language . . . by hanging out on the corners."

The program, hosted by Ted Koppel, featured two black American academics. Michael Eric Dyson, the author of the critical book on Cosby, was in debate with Shelby Steele, the author of several books on race relations. Koppel began by pointing out that the audience applauded when Cosby gave his controversial speech in Washington. Koppel said Cosby's speech had "resonance" and "truth to it [and] . . . doesn't presume to be a reflection of the entire picture."

Dyson said the audience in Washington for the *Brown* decision gala was filled with upper-class black Americans, and Cosby played to their discomfort about their poor brothers and sisters with remarks about poor blacks that were "bitter and acrimonious and vicious . . . part of a centuries-old tradition of the black elite looking down their noses and being embarrassed and ashamed by black people."

Steele turned the debate in exactly the opposite direction. He argued that since the civil rights movement, black Americans taking personal responsibility for their well-being is "the elephant in the living room that everybody for the last forty years has been looking away from. . . . we've made it taboo to talk about the words *black* and *responsibility* in the same breath." Later he added, "In black America we are asked by our leadership to constantly wear a mask which says that white people are responsible, and if you ask black people to be responsible you are blaming the victim. . . . Cosby crossed that line."

Dyson fired back that Cosby reinforced "right-wing, conservative values" and explained that "white America that is conservative wants to emphasize personal and individual responsibility when it is to their advantage." Steel answered, "The point remains . . . you cannot get out of poverty unless you take an enormous amount of personal responsibility for doing so. . . . Being the victim does not spare you from responsibility. . . . Responsibility is power."

The debate focused on Cosby, on white conservatives, and on taboo topics in black America. There is no debate, however, about the real crisis among the 24 percent of black Americans still locked in poverty and stuck in bad schools, who have limited opportunity to rise up the economic ladder.

If the debate had been a boxing match, Cosby would have been the knockout winner over his critics, as judged by the audience that first heard him in Washington, by the crowds that continue to come out to hear him around the nation, and by the people on the street who are asked about his bold stand. Ringside judges as varied as Jesse Jackson, Ted Koppel, and Shelby Steele gave Cosby the win.

At this point, Bill Cosby's legacy is not at risk. Poor people, especially the young, remain at risk, however. The challenge now is to get beyond the Cosby controversy and spell out concrete steps to lift people up, to bring them into the light. The big question remaining is: What is the next step?

10

WHAT NEXT?

ARRIVING AT REAL SOLUTIONS to help the poor get out of poverty is not as hard as it seems.

What is hard is getting the message out. It is especially hard when a deafening batch of shrill voices is shouting excuses for why the poor remain poor. It gets even more difficult when the culture celebrates the cycle of failure, anger, and self-defeating behavior that keeps poor black people shackled in the twenty-first century. And it becomes nearly impossible when smart, successful black people, under the banner of racial solidarity, refuse to hold poor black people responsible for their own failings.

For example, eighteen months after Bill Cosby tried to open a discussion of solutions to the crisis of persistent poverty in black America with his controversial speech, Michelle Singletary, a financial columnist, wrote in the *Washington Post* that Cosby was the problem. She complained that in his rush to call the poor to do better, he didn't even know the price of a teenager's sneakers.

In his Constitution Hall speech, Cosby expressed regret about parents who won't spend $250 to help their children become bet-

ter readers, but they will buy their children $500 sneakers. "All
this child knows is 'gimme, gimme, gimme,'" . . . these people are
not parenting," Cosby said.

In Singletary's opinion, Cosby was just "rattling off nonsense
much like his Fat Albert character Mushmouth." To show that
Cosby doesn't know what he is talking about, she quotes approv-
ingly from Michael Eric Dyson's anti-Cosby polemic. The columnist made Dyson's book the selection for her monthly book club.
She wrote that it devastated Cosby's claim that too many poor
black people throw away their money on high-priced, big-brand
consumer goods like fancy sneakers. In his book Dyson cites a
study of American buying patterns in which young white people
are found to be just as crazy about brand-name products as young
black people.

Singletary quoted a passage in which Dyson wrote that it was
elitist to hold poor black people to a higher standard than white
suburban kids who want to buy the latest sneakers. "It is interesting that Cosby expects poor parents and youth to be more fiscally
responsible than those with far greater resources prove to be,"
Dyson wrote. Dyson told Singletary in an interview for her column that Cosby's ideas made him guilty of "cruelty" to poor black
people.

Singletary and Dyson might want to look at a 2005 report
from Target Market. One eye-catching finding from the company, which tracks trends in consumer appetites, is that blacks
make up 12 percent of the population, but buy 30 percent of the
scotch sold in the United States. The report did not cover sneakers, but in comparison to whites of similar incomes, according to
a *USA Today* news story on the report, "blacks spend a significant
amount of their income on depreciable products." Similarly, a
2003 report on black investors found that white families saved 20

percent more per month than black families, even when their households had comparable incomes. Gee, it sounds like Cosby knew what he was talking about, after all.

Incredibly, in their rush to attack Cosby, Singletary and Dyson somehow miss the point that poor people have even less money than middle-class black people; that is why they are poor. And poor people have to be more cautious about how they spend their money if they want to survive. If the poor want to get out of poverty, they also have to save money that the middle class, black and white, might use to buy brand-name products, or go to a movie or out to dinner. And if the poor want to invest in their children, they have to make even more careful choices, including saving money that can then be spent on books, tutors, and learning experiences such as trips.

That might mean not buying expensive sneakers for a young person, but instead using that money to sharpen the child's reading skills by buying a reading program such as Hooked on Phonics. That is all Cosby was saying.

This is just plain old common sense. It applies to people of all races. It applies to the poor, the middle class, and even the rich who want to make the most of their money and build more wealth. If the poor could afford to buy brand-name sneakers, a big house, and Hooked on Phonics, there would not be a problem. But because they are not middle-class, they have to make tough choices that require deferred gratification if they want to get out of poverty. They have to get their priorities straight, and as far as Bill Cosby is concerned, the poor have to make educating children their top priority.

How the hell is it cruelty to say this out loud?

Speaking with me, Cosby had a simple question about the professor. "What is Dyson saying to make our people stronger?"

Cosby thinks he knows the answer. Dyson and other critics, he charges, "are afraid that they [won't be able to] frighten white people to give them money on the hustle."

Cosby's prescription for making the poor strong enough to help themselves may include some "castor-oil moments" such as telling a child that he or she can't have a pair of the latest Air Jordan sneakers. But bitter medicine is only spooned out by loving parents intent on helping a child grow strong. It is not about punishment.

The advice that Cosby is giving is time-tested. And it is arguably more important now because of the declining number of industrial jobs for people who might have strong backs but little education. That change in the American economy, as well as global competition for all jobs, has led to a dramatic change in how social classes are organized in the United States today. Fewer families of any race moved up the economic ladder over the last thirty years, according to the federal government. While the poor are struggling, families in the upper and middle classes are busy trying to keep their grip on financial security. They are investing more money in educating their children, even as the poor fall behind.

A *New York Times* series on the growing class divide in the nation found that an increasing percentage of the most successful students today are the children of the upper middle class and the rich. "Whatever children inherit from their parents—habits, skills, genes, contacts, money—seems to matter more today," and family structure becomes a class issue in modern America, too, according to the *Times*. The best-educated Americans now have fewer children. They also give birth to those children later in life, when they have more money to spend on the children. This is true for white parents, black parents, and immigrant parents. The gap between money earned by people who graduated from college and money earned by those who did not doubled in the last twenty years. It is becoming harder for the poor to compete.

The good news is that there is a formula for getting out of poverty today. The magical steps begin with finishing high school, but finishing college is much better. Step number two is taking a job and holding it. Step number three is marrying after finishing school and while you have a job. And the final step to give yourself the best chance to avoid poverty is to have children only after you are twenty-one and married. This formula applies to black people and white people alike.

The poverty rate for any black man or woman who follows that formula is 6.4 percent. The overall poverty rate for black Americans, based on 2002 census data, the year this analysis was done, was 21.5 percent. In other words, by meeting those basic requirements, black Americans can cut their chances of being poor by two-thirds. This is a consistent pattern. By 2004 the poverty rate for any black man or woman who follows that formula is only 5.8 percent. That compares to an overall poverty rate of 24.7 percent for black people in 2004. Another way to look at it is that a black family that does not meet the requirements will more than triple their chances of being poor. Even white American families have a higher poverty rate (7.8 percent) than black people who finished high school, got married, had children after 21, and worked for at least one week a year.

These magical steps to a middle-class life were first laid out in a study by the American Enterprise Institute. "Among adult males with just a high school education of all races, 91 percent had family incomes greater than twice the poverty level," wrote Charles Murray in the 1986 study, "According to Age: Longitudinal Profiles of AFDC Recipients and the Poor by Age Group." Murray concluded that "if you are a male in this country, being poor is not easy." The formula also works for black women who want to avoid poverty, with special emphasis on one key—not having a baby outside of marriage.

A 2002 report from the Institute for American Values, a non-partisan group that studies families, concluded that "marriage is an issue of paramount importance if we wish to help the most vulnerable members of our society: the poor, minorities, and children." The statistical evidence for that claim is strong. Research shows that in 2002 most black children, 68 percent, were born to unwed mothers. Those numbers have real consequences. For example, 35 percent of black women who had a child out of wedlock live in poverty. Only 17 percent of married black women overall are in poverty. In a 2005 report the institute concluded, "Economically, marriage for black Americans is a wealth-creating and poverty-reducing institution. The marital status of African American parents is one of the most powerful determinants of the economic status of African American families."

The report also found tremendous benefits in marriage for men. A married man earns at least 10 percent more and as much as 40 percent more than a single man with the same education and job history. Married black men also live longer and are more likely to report that they are "very happy."

The authors noted that over the last fifty years, basically the period after the *Brown* decision, "the percentage of black families headed by married couples declined from 78 percent to 34 percent." In the thirty years from 1950 to 1980, households headed by black women who never married jumped from 3.8 per thousand to 69.7 per thousand. That, too, had real consequences. In 1940, 75 percent of black children lived with both parents. By 1990 only 33 percent of black children lived with a mom and dad—"largely a result of marked increases in the number of never-married black mothers." And there is no question about the impact on black children. With both parents in the house, they do better in school; the children of married people also have fewer run-ins with the police, as well as better self-esteem, and are more likely to enter into marriage before having children. This is a cycle of success creating more success and prosperity.

"For policymakers who care about black America, marriage matters," wrote the authors of the report, a group of black scholars. They called marriage in black America an important strategy for "improving the well-being of African Americans and for strengthening civil society."

Here is Cosby at an October 2004 town-hall meeting in Milwaukee: "It is not all right for your fifteen-year-old daughter to have a child," he told black parents. "I'm not talking to you any different from a grandfather who would say, 'I wouldn't do that if I were you.'"

A few days after his controversial speech in May 2004, Cosby wrote in the *Los Angeles Times* that "we don't need another federal commission to study the problem [of black poverty]. Scholars such as W.E.B. DuBois and John Hope Franklin . . . have already written eloquently on the subject. What we need now is parents sitting down with children, overseeing homework, sending children off to school in the morning well fed, clothed, and ready to learn."

None of this is a matter of arguing over morality, blaming the poor, or excusing "the system" and its racism. Instead, Cosby and the academics are telling poor black people about sure-fire strategies for helping themselves and their families. There is no argument about the facts. If any person, including a black child born in poverty, will go as far as possible in school and show a willingness to work, he will be rewarded with enough money in his pocket to make it almost certain he will never get caught in poverty. If he also builds on the foundation of a strong marriage before having children, he will be rewarded: He will have even more money in his pocket, children who aspire to do well in school, and greatly reduced likelihood of seeing his children in trouble with drugs or having a run-in with the police that leads to jail.

Timely information is critical to success in war and business. Understanding the importance of education, marriage, and parenting to black families today is critical for any young black person trying to chart a course for a successful life. It is particularly important when so many young black women continue to have children outside of marriage. Do they understand what they are doing to themselves, to their children, to their chances for being happy?

They might not understand that they are hurting themselves, according to two Philadelphia sociologists. In a book titled *Promises I Can Keep*, the academics found that poor single women of all races consistently told them that having a baby need not be connected to marriage. The reason is that the poor women said they generally did not want to be the wives of the poorly educated, controlling, even abusive men whom they identified as the men most commonly found in low-income neighborhoods. Most important, it is hard for these young women to see those young men as stable fathers and reliable providers for a family, so they conclude there is no downside to having the baby without a husband.

William Galston, a professor of public policy at the University of Maryland, claims to understand the logic of these poor young women. "If I were a woman . . . and the pool of men I was looking at involved dropouts with criminal records and abusive patterns, I wouldn't marry, either," he told Bill Raspberry, a columnist at the *Washington Post*. "But that omits a prior question: Why would I allow such a man to impregnate me?"

The answer is that these poor women are acting on a massive error in reasoning. Their mistake leads to a lifetime of bad consequences for the child and the mother. Obviously the message about the magical powers of the formula—not having children until they are twenty-one, married, and graduated from high school—is not getting through to these young women. They think they can provide love and money for the child, as well as a peaceful home, without a man, especially the unreliable men they encounter most easily in the neighborhood.

Galston is convinced the poor know all about what the good life looks like, from college graduation to a good car and a nice house with a picket fence. But the poor are missing information on how to get the good life, he said. The poor don't know "what to do next," is the way Galston puts it.

And obviously they are not getting that information from American popular culture's caricature of authentic blackness as a violent, oversexed, materialistic, uneducated person living the "thug" life. The message from TV to young black people is that they can be true to their community by putting on an angry attitude, dismissing school as a waste of time, speaking broken English, wearing flashy clothes and gold teeth, and putting dazzling rims on their rides. That bilious message clearly has nothing to say about achieving a lifetime of financial success and good relationships, and putting their children on a good path.

That is why it is important for someone of Bill Cosby's stature to take a risk to get the message out about the road to economic salvation—education, families, and good parenting. That is why it is more than fair for Cosby to proclaim for all the world to hear that poor black people whose children are dropping out of high school, whose daughters are having babies out of wedlock, whose sons are filling up the jails, are not taking advantage of the doors that have opened since the *Brown* decision. When it comes to creating the good life themselves, too many of the poor are acting against their own best interests—they are hurting themselves and the black community.

Why? Again, the heart of the answer is that the poor are not getting important information from civil rights leaders, from politicians, and from their culture (their music, their movies, their fashion). There is no trusted source with a pulpit or a microphone telling people in need about the path to a better life. There is no one calling this situation a crisis. That is why it was so exceptional for Cosby to raise his voice and say to poor black people "we didn't come from giving up . . . we came from surviving!"

The nation's leading civil rights groups are missing in action in this effort to get out the good news. They claim to be too busy to get the message out. They are locked into arguing that "the system" is causing the continued high level of poverty in black America. Their goal seems to be to get government money for programs, grants, and scholarships for the black community. That money has done some good. But at this point a blind pursuit of government money to help the poor is a tired, failed strategy. It encourages patterns of dependency among black people. It leads to cynicism about what has become of the civil rights movement. In its finest hour the movement appealed to the conscience of the nation, to its ideals, by seeking justice. Now the movement has descended to using racial guilt trips, basically to extort government money for bigger budgets for programs that show no sign of working. The disdain for this shadow of a formerly great movement is so deep that many Americans, including Cosby, identify these black leaders with their hands out on behalf of the poor as "poverty pimps."

There is no discounting the damage done by slavery and racism. They are a tragically heavy weight of history on black people. And while much of the burden has lifted, it can still be found weighing on black people, through stereotypes and negative images, leaving us at a real disadvantage. But with the *Brown* decision and the passage of civil rights and voting rights laws, the historic damage done by slavery and racism is no longer heavy enough to stop most black people from fighting through the static and making their way to a better life.

Somehow the reduced burden of racism over the last fifty years has escaped the attention of civil rights leaders. They have become detached from the reality of the lives of poor black people in their preoccupation with the history of racism. They have also lost the trust of much of white America by failing to speak honestly about the baggage of self-defeating behavior that is hamstringing too many poor black people. In the aftermath of Hurricane Katrina, *Time* magazine's Joe Klein wrote that the attempt by black leaders to "make gains by browbeating white people and ignoring the responsibility of the 'victims' themselves has been a total loser." Klein tied that failed approach to the low standing of the Democratic Party, and said the black leadership's anger is "irrelevant" to the question of how to create opportunities for the poor and generate support across the board, in all communities, for helping those in need.

The answer to the question of how to create opportunities for the poor is to get them to take school seriously—to set high academic expectations for their children and to insist on high expectations from teachers in good schools. It is also a personal matter of self-control that begins with understanding the power of the family and putting love, romance, and children (as well as knowing how to be good parents) in their proper order. Conservative writer Linda Chavez, the former head of the U.S. Civil Rights Commission, said after Hurricane Katrina that the "chief cause of poverty today among blacks is no longer racism—it is the breakdown of the traditional family." Critics call this "blaming the poor." They say this answer puts pressure on the poor. They say this with a straight face, even though nearly 70 percent of black children are born to single women, damning a high number of them to poverty, bad schools, and bad influences. They say this knowing that in 1964, in a far more hostile and racist America,

82 percent of black households had both parents in place and close to half of those households owned a business.

This is not about blaming anyone. A better way to think about the matter is to say that the poor can be empowered to help themselves. And once the poor have been transformed into powerful, positive advocates for their own rescue, they can be a voice for organizing, for building coalitions across racial lines to acquire better schools and better social programs, and for supporting politicians who understand the struggle to get out of poverty's grip. This is authentic black empowerment in keeping with the grand tradition of self-determination going back to black Americans who fought before, during, and after slavery to be recognized as full citizens of the republic with equal rights, opportunities, and responsibilities.

Yet, somehow, reality is being twisted. The people being held up as role models and lauded as "authentically black" are the people dropping out of school, ending up as gang-bangers and hustlers, having babies as unmarried teens. Those people should be run out of town. Here is how Bill Cosby put it in his famous speech: "These people are not funny anymore. They're faking and they're dragging me way down because the state, the city, and all these people have to pick up the tab on them because they don't want to accept that they have to study to get an education."

What is really crazy is that while the people who are defeating themselves are being celebrated in this distorted picture, the black middle class is being put down. This is the black middle class that has taken advantage of new opportunities created by the *Brown* decision. This is the black middle class that has followed the formula of education and family and hard work. These are people who don't have the advantages of the white middle class, but are still climbing. They rely more heavily than the white middle class on earned income—their paychecks—because they have less money that comes from inheritance, savings, real estate, and investments. Living on paychecks, most people in that black middle class are engaged in a valiant struggle to keep their jobs and families together to avoid falling back into poverty. Their hard work, however, does not protect them from being libeled as people who are acting as if they were better than poor black people, as if they have forgotten where they came from and don't care about black people whom the economy has been left behind.

Bill Cosby calls this the "Bourgeois Baiting Business." He told me his story of growing up poor in Philadelphia. It was generally a loving neighborhood. But when public welfare gave out free eyeglasses to poor children, the city-issued glasses all came with the same clear plastic frames. Self-conscious children would mock anyone who wore the clear-framed glasses as poor, even though they were all relatively poor. It was the same story when someone was evicted and their furniture was put out on the street. Some insecure neighbors would mock those who had been evicted, even though they were all close to poor. The same element of self-hate from the poor prompts them to put down people who are working their way up the economic ladder, complaining that their hard work and sacrifice are old-fashioned and pretentious.

Earl Ofari Hutchinson, president of the Los Angeles Urban Policy Roundtable, speaking on the National Public Radio program *News and Notes with Ed Gordon*, said a greedy black middle class is putting its energy into making itself richer and has "a blind spot to . . . the needs of the poor." He said the black middle class puts its emphasis on programs that will help the black middle class, programs such as "affirmative action, business opportunities, professional opportunities, electing more black Democrats to office." Hutchinson later added that black leadership, in politics and culture, is pursuing a "middle-class point of view, the upwardly mobile point of view, the business and professional point of view . . . a leadership that ignores, in terms of a comprehensive agenda, the poorest of the poor."

And what is this self-serving black middle class failing to do to help the black poor? Apparently, critics such as Hutchinson feel the black middle class is not sufficiently involved in pressuring the government for more poverty programs. This grubby black middle class has its eyes set on moving up, by Hutchinson's account, so it does not buy enough homes in low-income black neighborhoods, is not opening businesses there, and is not sending its children to schools with poor children. What the critics are missing is that the black middle class today is made up of people who are often the first in their families to have college degrees. They are competing in a tough global economy to hold jobs, to start businesses, and to raise families. They are pressed to build wealth through savings and investments with little or no inheritance. They are often part of families where cousins and aunts, if not parents, ask for help from anyone in the family who makes it into that maligned black middle class.

And the black middle class is all the while pushing against a very hard ceiling that has kept black people from top jobs in business, nonprofits, government, and media. Doors have opened to create new opportunities. But education and skills are required to succeed once the opportunity is offered. And even the most talented black person has to deal with stereotypes about lack of intelligence, drive, and the ability to be part of the team. All of that corporate culture of racism is very much alive and weighing on black people inside the doors of opportunity. The idea of diversity and affirmative action has been spread to white women, the disabled, gays, and more. If a middle-class black person operating in today's economic climate gets a chance to move to a better neighborhood or send his children to a better school, he should be congratulated as a trail-blazer, not condemned as an Uncle Tom.

In an interview for this book, Cosby asked how the Salvation Army, Boys Clubs of America, and United Way agencies are paid for if they are not supported by the middle class, black and white.

But what if, in the name of reaching back to help their poor brothers and sisters, every middle-class black person in America stopped trying to keep their heads above water and focused on the 24 percent of African Americans in poverty? What if they abandoned what Hutchinson calls the "upwardly mobile point of view"? The black middle class could then join together to pressure the federal government to increase funding for social programs specifically targeted at poor black people. This approach reveals a naïve trust in the ability of government programs to help the poor and defeat the hard, entrenched poverty remaining in black America.

Trusting the government to help the black poor also flies in the face of history. It is in contradiction to the sad track record of government programs for the poor, such as public housing expansion during the 1970s. Any poor family that looked to old-style public housing for help often had to contend with crime-ridden housing projects that isolated the poor. It not only isolated the poor, but compacted poverty with race and neighborhood. It gave poverty an address, a specific location, where the poor were subject to different standards of low-level treatment from the police, supermarkets, and schools. It was a combustible mix that has condemned generations of poor black people to a living hell. Those units are now being torn down nationwide as city after city acknowledges the failed idea of helping the poor by essentially concentrating them in warehouses.

And that is not the only failure. How about increases in school funding that have resulted in more excuses for poor test scores and higher dropout rates, and have led to a national lack of faith in big-city public schools? How about more-generous welfare programs that pushed black men out of the house in the 1960s and led to a dramatic rise in out-of-wedlock births? Here is Illinois's black Democratic senator Barack Obama on the Senate floor after Hurricane Katrina: "I hope we realize that the people of New Orleans weren't just abandoned during the hurricane. They were abandoned long ago to murder and mayhem in the streets, to substandard schools, to dilapidated housing, to inadequate health care, to a pervasive sense of hopelessness." In other words, they were abandoned and isolated by corrupt, ineffective government programs despite all the progress made by a civil rights revolution.

John McWhorter, the author and conservative social critic, believes the "black ghetto" that is now accepted as normal in American cities is really only forty years old, about as old as the government's first stab at welfare reform. He argues that those changes in welfare transformed a safety-net program into a program that paid people more money to have children than to have a nine-to-five job, particularly if the mothers did not have a husband, especially one with a job, in the house. McWhorter calls that kind of federal legislation "well-intended but disastrous policies aimed at inner cities." He makes the case that it "created a new kind of poor black American" that replaced segregated but stable neighborhoods of people who worked. It also replaced small businesses, from barber shops to handymen, who formed the backbone of a society focused on moving up the economic ladder and not on when a government check was arriving in the mailbox.

The opposite point of view comes, surprisingly, from a liberal social critic, Patricia Rose, a professor of American Studies at the University of California–Santa Cruz. She agrees with the conservative McWhorter that government policies aimed at getting people out of poverty have had negative results and essentially created the post-*Brown* decision ghetto where deeply entrenched poverty has less to do with race than with being caught in a culture of poverty.

But the reason for the culture of poverty, according to Rose, is racism in how the government doled out money under its key social programs, such as Social Security and the GI Bill. While those federal plans helped whites get out of poverty, get a house, and get an education, Rose contends, the federal government often discriminated against black people seeking their fair share of the money made available under those programs. That put white Americans at an advantage and left black Americans farther behind both educationally and economically, resulting in the 24-percent black poverty rate of today, a rate three times higher than the poverty rate among whites. Even the urban renewal programs of the 1960s, she argues, were intended to help blacks but "gutted access to affordable housing and other resources in the cities." This thesis is explored in detail in a book titled *When Affirmative Action Was White*, by Ira Katznelson.

In the aftermath of Hurricane Katrina, Rose and McWhorter appeared together on *Talk of the Nation*, a National Public Radio show. Although they agree government policies have failed the poor, owing to ineptitude or racism or both, they were positioned as smart black people with opposite views of the cause of the tragically high poverty rate in black New Orleans. In that setting they did not emphasize their agreement on the damage done by government policies intended to help the poor. Instead they focused on their disagreement about why, as President Reagan once said, "we fought a war on poverty and poverty won."

Rose presented the idea that black poverty is the result of "systemic" failure by the government and ongoing racism in American culture. "If we don't take history seriously and [the economic repercussions of racism on] our current policies we're not going to solve this problem." She discounted the power of the

Brown decision and the civil rights legislation of the 1960s that supposedly opened doors to people of color. Some doors did open, but in reality the government continued to be racially biased, even though it claimed to be race-neutral and to give an equal opportunity to all. For example, she cites the disparity between good schools for mostly white children in the suburbs and bad schools for mostly black children in the cities. Repairing the damage done to black people by racially biased government programs, she said, requires admitting the impact of the history of racism. That admission will obligate the federal government to spend more to help the people most damaged by the racist past, today's black poor.

McWhorter responded that Rose is going to wait a long time for apologies and to find "utopia when people need help now." While many Americans may wish for a change in the political winds and better support for the poor by the government, there is no indication from Democrats or Republicans of major new poverty legislation aimed at uplifting poor minorities. There is no sign of an imminent end to all racism, complete with apologies. With no hint of a "New Deal" or "Great Society" enterprise about to be launched, McWhorter raises an important question: What are people who genuinely care about black poverty to do until the day that the lion lies down with the lamb, racism is ended, and there is a level playing field for all Americans on which the poor are given all they need to succeed?

The obvious answer is for people to take every possible step possible right now to take care of themselves and help their families. This is not letting the government off the hook so much as dealing with real solutions to the immediate needs of real people. No one is arguing that problems with past government programs are a reason to give up and stop asking the government to lend a hand to the poor. The fact of the failure of government programs—agreed upon by both the left and the right in the person of Rose and McWhorter—does, however, point to the importance of finding successful strategies beyond government. There are steps that individuals can take to help themselves. Once again, those strategies begin with getting a high school education, not having children until one is twenty-one and married, working hard at any job, and being good parents.

Once that is settled, then the conversation extends to helping the growing number of working poor people. They deserve to do more than scrape by for their forty hours of work a week. Polls show that Americans of all political stripes believe that anyone who works full time should make enough to stay out of poverty. Political coalitions can be built to better support existing anti-poverty programs and stir up new legislation to make sure that working people can get reliable, affordable transportation, child care, access to a doctor, new dollars for big-city schools, a living wage, and subsidized housing that is mixed into middle-class and upper-class neighborhoods. Getting people out of poor neighborhoods is a proven formula for giving them a better life. In Chicago, a successful suit was filed in the 1960s by black public housing residents asking for an end to public policy of being segregated in poverty by the city government. That led to a program to move them into mixed-income housing in other parts of the city and suburbs. The result of these people's getting out of an enforced ghetto of poor black people and moving into the mainstream was higher grade point averages, higher graduation rates, and higher numbers graduating from college. Employment and income also went up for the adults. In that political environment it is also possible to argue for increasing the Earned Income Tax Credit to further reward hardworking people in low-paying jobs.

Across every racial and class line, in every shade of Republican and Democrat, Americans agree that the working poor should be assured that getting up and going to work is better than staying at home and waiting for welfare.

At the moment, these are all good ideas, but they have gone nowhere in Congress or the White House under Democrats and Republicans, and their prospects for the near future are not good. As Jason DeParle wrote in *American Dream* (his book on welfare reform that tracked the lives of three women), the poor are currently so lost in living from moment to moment and in political apathy that they don't "lobby or sue . . . march or riot."

It is no insult to the poor, and it is not blaming the poor, to say that the poor, once they take basic steps to help themselves, are strong enough to join in organized political action to show the larger society—including the most conservative elected officials—that they are ready to add to American productivity, wealth, and success. Building broad political support for poverty programs begins with acknowledging the poor as intelligent, ambitious people who are capable of helping themselves.

That is where Bill Cosby comes in.

He is starting this process of political empowerment by trumpeting the news that there is much that poor black people can do for themselves—and immediately—to boost their fortunes and become both self-supporting and politically strong. The process starts with the very themes that Cosby highlighted in his *Brown* decision speech. You begin, he said, by being good parents, by paying attention to your child and to how that child is doing in school, and by demanding good schools. He insisted that children be told to speak proper English because it is the foundation for success in school and beyond. These are basic investments in the power of the next generation.

In an interview for this book, Cosby recounted a speaking visit he made to a big city during which some public officials arranged for him to meet with three bright young ninth-graders. All three came from a troubled neighborhood, but all had reputations as good kids, young people who were respectful and went to school and avoided gangs. But when Cosby asked them what they were learning in school, none of the boys could do better than say they had a history class, a math class, and a science class. Cosby asked what they were studying in the classes, but the boys could not say.

"I looked at all three—and the gentleman who brought them up to the hotel—and I said 'Do you see what I see?'" Cosby recalled. "Obviously, nothing is happening at home for these kids. They couldn't even bullshit about what was going on in school. If they had any protection from adults at home, the first thing that adult will ask them when they come home is 'What did you learn in school today?' So the boys learn that they have got to have something to say when they get home to answer that question, so they have to pay attention. These kids couldn't do it."

Cosby also called on fathers to know their children and spend time with them so that the children feel loved and know they are valued by their family as a basis for feeling they are worthy of success in the world. He spoke up in defense of the daring souls who speak out against teenagers having babies and women having babies with different men but without husbands. Cosby said plainly that having children under those conditions weakens families, makes children unstable, and increases poverty.

He asked people to invest in their neighborhoods by not putting up with crime, even if it is committed by their own children or the boy next door. He called for poor people to get guns out of their community. "We've got to take the neighborhood back," he said. He told neighbors to watch out for all the children in the community and not be "scared" to tell the parents and the police when children are running wild. Cosby risks saying that people in prison are not heroes and that it is cancerous for a culture to accept prison as a natural stop for any growing young man. And he pointed a damning finger at multimillionaire black athletes who can't read and who dress like thugs. They are not heroes, either. They are harmful, self-indulgent personalities who advertise bad values to black children who look up to these athletes as successful, black male role models.

Cosby, a sixty-nine-year-old who has no need for publicity or money, nevertheless jumped in front of a fast train fueled by big money—American culture—and tried to save poor black people from being run over by racist, minstrel-show images of them-selves as violent, stupid, and self-hating thugs. He put himself on the line when he called for the church to get involved, to "hit the streets" and speak proudly of Christian values and proudly hold up people with good character who are successful.

Cosby stood up that night in Washington in the name of cre-ating powerful people who can pick up on the black American tra-ditions of self-determination and self-empowerment. He even put his standing with other black leaders at risk when he asked black people not to respond to leaders who are just trying to make a buck by using their poverty to get a cut of a government poverty program.

This is Cosby's love song to black America. It is the gift of truth. Now it up to poor people, to black people, to Ameri-cans who care about issues of race and poverty, to begin the most successful antipoverty program in American history by ac-cepting the riches of Cosby's gift and acting to make the poor powerful.

ACKNOWLEDGMENTS

This book grew out of discussions with two smart editors, Chris Jackson and Steve Ross.

Unlike my other books, which are histories about the black American experience, I had to find a more personal voice in writing about contemporary events. Chris Jackson had just the right touch and vision to bring this book out of me. And Steve Ross stood firmly behind the book at every turn. When Chris Jackson took a new position, Rachel Klayman embraced the book with tremendous spirit and became its champion. Thanks, Rachel.

Robert Barnett, my lawyer and friend, believed in this book from early on. His dedication was combined with wise counsel along the way. Thank you very much.

Christian Nwachukwu Jr. came to the rescue to help with research and editorial assistance. A 2004 graduate of Morehouse College, his knowledge of contemporary black culture and dedication to the idea of improving life for all Americans became a part of the fabric of this work. Mary Glendinning, reference librarian at National Public Radio, was intrepid, smart, and helpful—the best. Kee Malesky and other library staff, particularly Alphonse Vinh, always pointed me in the right direction.

My special thanks to Ellen McDonnell, the leader of NPR's *Morning Edition*, who gave me the leeway to write this book while continuing my work as a senior correspondent.

It is hard to give enough thanks to Bill Cosby. His daring

speech was the spark for this book. David Brokaw, Cosby's talent agent, acted as a bridge to Bill Cosby and even more, as a guide to the twists and turns of the debate over Cosby's famous speech.

Thanks to David Brand, a true wise man of American life. My heart goes out to Armstrong Williams, my friend and guide through Washington life. Robert Traynham, Ron Walters, Joseph Watkins, and Tara Wahl are my political insiders. My friend Donna Brazile is a rare combination. She is always keen and honest in her assessment of ideas and people but knows how to play hardball, partisan politics with the best.

The constant support from my friends at the American Program Bureau is deeply appreciated. Special thanks to Perry Steinberg and Robert Walker.

My friends and colleagues at NPR gave me more than a little help and lots of enthusiasm. Our leaders—Kevin Klose, Ken Stern, Jay Kernis, Barbara Rehm, and Bill Marimow. And my pals—Alex Chadwick, Audrey Wynn, Steve Inskeep, Scott Simon, Jim Wallace, Madeleine Brand, Renee Montagne, Michele Norris, Cara Gerhard, Melissa Block, Bruce Auster, Sarah Mobley-Smith, David Folkenflick, Cheryl Hampton, Pamela Duckett, Susan Feeney, Gwen Thompkins, Ron Elving, John Buckley, Parris Morgan, Ken Rudin, Victor Holliday, Jordana Hochman, Walter Ray Watson, Emily Barocas, Lisa Chow, Brakkton Booker, Kevin Langley, Dalia Martinez, Vincent Muse, James Hodge, Doreen McCallister, Melinda Weir, Margaret West, Devar Ardalan, Neva Grant, Ed Gordon, Vladimir Dubinsky, Steve Murno, Jim Wildman, Christine Arrasmith, Wilma Counsul, Deborah Berry, Meike Buxton, Ben Bergman, Bridget Kelley, Dianna Douglas, Barry Gordemer, Claudette Haberman, Joel Riddle, Julia Bailey, Taylor Ford, Jacob Conrad, Christopher Johnson, and Neal Carruth.

My friends at Fox always gave encouragement: Roger Ailes, John Moody, Bill Shine, Brit Hume, Chris Wallace, Bill O'Reilly, Kim Hume, Marty Ryan, Shepherd Smith, Greta Van Susteren, Bruce Becker, Mara Liasson, Fred Barnes, Robert Novak, Mort Kondrake, Querry Robinson, Laurie Luhn, Cory Howard, Alex Finland, Brian Doherty, Walter Carter, Molly Henneberg, Christina Svolopoulos, Victoria Royer, Julie Zann, Shona Allison, Tony Snow, Andy Och, Rick DiBella, Andrea DeVito, Brigitte Lyles, Michele Remillard, Mary Ellen Tasillo, Debra DeFrank, Stacia Lynds, Tracey Madorma, and Mary Pat Dennert.

Sincere appreciation to the best of friends: Gabe Mehretaab, Jerrilynn Ness, Pat Richter, Bess Rothenberg, Bill Raspberry, Carol Post, Father John Harmon, Sec. Alphonso Jackson, Marcia Jackson, Chris Cowan, Nancie McPhail, Cheryl Gibert, Byron Lewis Sr., Byron Lewis Jr., Courtland Milloy, Dante James, Fritz Bech, Lucille Blair, Jim Hudson, Bill and Cynthianna Lightfoot, Jenny Pond, Barrett Nnoka, Patrick Herald, Charlotte Hoffman, Diane Thomson, and James Loadholt.

My brother and sister, Roger and Elena, are still showing me the way. Arthur and Minna West, Scooter and Lethia West, along with Ginger Macomber, Beat Jenny, Ligia and Jonathan Mason, fill the family with love as reflected in the faces of Jonathan, Alexandra, Marissa, Ashley, Christopher, Paul, and Chip.

And, of course, there is no way to say how grateful I am for the love of my delightful family, my greatest blessing: Delise, Antonio, Regan, and Raphael. God bless.

Long life and love to all—I'll take the responsibility.

INDEX

Also by JUAN WILLIAMS

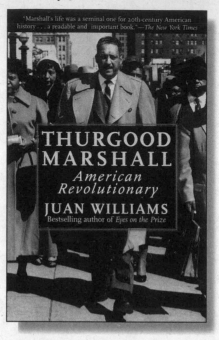

"Marshall's life was a seminal one for twentieth-century
American history. . . . A readable and important book."
—*New York Times*

"Magisterial . . . In Williams's richly detailed portrait,
Marshall emerges as a born rebel."
—*Time*

"Compelling . . . This is a full-blooded account of a remarkable man."
—*Seattle Post-Intelligencer*

A *New York Times* Notable Book of the Year

THURGOOD MARSHALL

978-0-8129-3299-7

$16.00 paper (Canada: $24.00)

Available from Three Rivers Press wherever books are sold.